HEATH
MIDDLE LEVEL
LITERATURE

Out of Tune

Conflicts develop for many different reasons—in families, schools, or communities. What do you do when things don't go right?

AUTHORS

Donna Alvermann
Linda Miller Cleary
Kenneth Donelson
Donald Gallo
Alice Haskins
J. Howard Johnston
John Lounsbury
Alleen Pace Nilsen
Robert Pavlik
Jewell Parker Rhodes
Alberto Alvaro Ríos
Sandra Schurr
Lyndon Searfoss
Julia Thomason
Max Thompson
Carl Zon

D.C. Heath and Company
Lexington, Massachusetts / Toronto, Ontario

STAFF CREDITS

EDITORIAL Barbara A. Brennan, Helen Byers, Christopher Johnson, Kathleen Kennedy Kelley, Owen Shows, Rita M. Sullivan
Proofreading: JoAnne B. Sgroi

CONTRIBUTING WRITERS Nance Davidson, Florence Harris

SERIES DESIGN Robin Herr

BOOK DESIGN Caroline Bowden, Daniel Derdula, Susan Geer, Diana Maloney, Angela Sciaraffa, Bonnie Chayes Yousefian
Art Editing: Carolyn Langley

PHOTOGRAPHY *Series Photography Coordinator:* Carmen Johnson
Photo Research Supervisor: Martha Friedman
Photo Researchers: Wendy Enright, Linda Finigan, Po-yee McKenna, PhotoSearch, Inc., Gillian Speeth, Denise Theodores
Assignment Photography Coordinators: Susan Doheny, Gayna Hoffman, Shawna Johnston

COMPUTER PREPRESS Ricki Pappo, Kathy Meisl
Richard Curran, Michele Locatelli

PERMISSIONS Dorothy B. McLeod

PRODUCTION Patrick Connolly

Cover: *Enigmatic Combat* Arshile Gorky; 1936-38, oil on canvas 35 3/4" x 48", San Francisco Museum of Modern Art, gift of Jeanne Reynal. **Cover Design:** Steve Snider

International Standard Book Number: 0-669-32100-1 (soft cover); 0-669-38170-5 (hard cover)
2 3 4 5 6 7 8 9 10-RRD-99 98 97 96 95 94

Middle Level Authors

Donna Alvermann, University of Georgia
Alice Haskins, Howard County Public Schools, Maryland
J. Howard Johnston, University of South Florida
John Lounsbury, Georgia College
Sandra Schurr, University of South Florida
Julia Thomason, Appalachian State University
Max Thompson, Appalachian State University
Carl Zon, California Assessment Collaborative

Literature and Language Arts Authors

Linda Miller Cleary, University of Minnesota
Kenneth Donelson, Arizona State University
Donald Gallo, Central Connecticut State University
Alleen Pace Nilsen, Arizona State University
Robert Pavlik, Cardinal Stritch College, Milwaukee
Jewell Parker Rhodes, Arizona State University
Alberto Alvaro Ríos, Arizona State University
Lyndon Searfoss, Arizona State University

Teacher Consultants

Suzanne Aubin, Patapsco Middle School, Ellicott City, Maryland
Judy Baxter, Newport News Public Schools, Newport News, Virginia
Saundra Bryn, Director of Research and Development, El Mirage, Arizona
Lorraine Gerhart, Elmbrook Middle School, Elm Grove, Wisconsin
Kathy Tuchman Glass, Burlingame Intermediate School, Burlingame, California
Lisa Mandelbaum, Crocker Middle School, Hillsborough, California
Lucretia Pannozzo, John Jay Middle School, Katonah, New York
Carol Schultz, Jerling Junior High, Orland Park, Illinois
Jeanne Siebenman, Grand Canyon University, Phoenix, Arizona
Gail Thompson, Garey High School, Pomona, California
Rufus Thompson, Grace Yokley School, Ontario, California
Tom Tufts, Conniston Middle School, West Palm Beach, Florida
Edna Turner, Harpers Choice Middle School, Columbia, Maryland
C. Anne Webb, Buerkle Junior High School, St. Louis, Missouri
Geri Yaccino, Thompson Junior High School, St. Charles, Illinois

CONTENTS

THE LITERATURE

ASKING BIG QUESTIONS ABOUT THE LITERATURE

PROJECTS

1 WRITING WORKSHOP
CONVINCE THEM WITH A LETTER   106-111

Persuade two opposing groups that there's a way to resolve their conflict.

2 COOPERATIVE LEARNING
A TV GUIDE FOR PARENTS   112-113

Make a TV guide that will help parents analyze TV sitcoms and evaluate which ones offer positive role models to young viewers.

3 HELPING YOUR COMMUNITY
WORDS OF ADVICE   114-115

How would you settle an argument with a friend? What's the best way to reach agreement in a group? Your conflict resolution manual can be just what others need.

Picture This

Imagine this predicament. You've been wanting to know a certain group of kids, but they've never seemed very friendly before. Now they've invited you to do something after school—but something you don't feel right about. You don't want to say yes, but if you say no, the group might not include you again. What do you feel? Conflict. What can you do? You can try to ignore your inner struggle. Or you can take steps to resolve it. No one likes conflict, but we all experience it at times. It can help to know there are different types of conflict—as well as strategies for trying to resolve them.

1 Pick a picture.

These photographs depict different sorts of conflict: people at odds with nature or with each other. Look at each picture carefully and speculate about what's happening in it. Then describe each picture in your journal as though you're watching its drama unfold. Describe how each conflict looks as well as how it feels to the person(s) experiencing it.

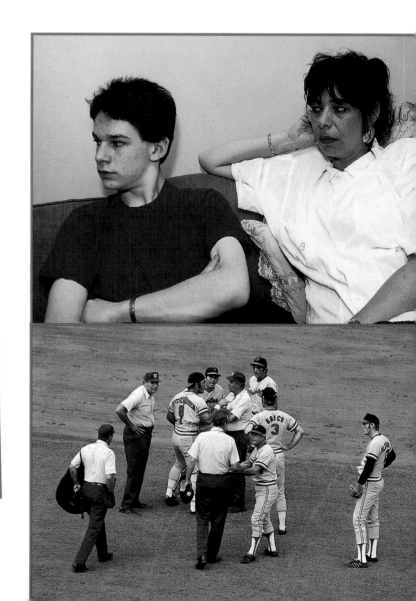

Discuss the conflict.

With a partner or a small group, compare notes about each photograph by discussing these questions:

- What might have caused this conflict?

- How does each person feel about his or her part in the conflict as it's happening? Afterward?

- What could be the immediate results of each party's actions? What might the later consequences be?

- What choices might each party have for dealing with the conflict?

Role-play the alternatives.

With your partner or small group, select one photograph and role-play the conflict and a possible resolution. Then dramatize it a second time, with another resolution. Discuss which option seems best to you, and why.

Asking Big Questions About the Theme

What causes conflict?

In your journal, make a web like this one. Let your mind wander to words and phrases for things you consider to be causes of conflict between people. Write them inside circles around the central phrase. Then compare your web to a classmate's.

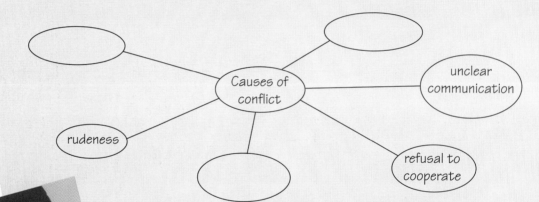

What are the different kinds of conflict?

With the whole class, brainstorm different kinds of conflict. Then discuss each kind of conflict and classify it according to these categories: *person against person, person against nature, person against society,* or *person against self.*

How do individuals and groups resolve conflicts?

With a partner, collect newspaper and magazine articles about local, national, and international conflicts. Then fill out a chart like this one. Discuss patterns in conflict resolution that you notice.

Title of Article	People Involved	Conflict	Cause	Actions Taken	Result and Consequences

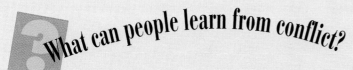

What can people learn from conflict?

Think of a past conflict you learned something from. In your journal, briefly summarize the conflict and write about what it taught you. Then explain how differently you might react to the same conflict if you experienced it today.

NOW Think!

Suppose you've been asked to serve on a conflict resolution committee at school. What kinds of skills and strategies do you need in order to help individuals and groups in conflict? As you read the literature selections in this unit, see whether your ideas about skills and strategies for conflict resolution grow and change.

Amanda and the

Lithograph from *L'ordre des oiseaux*, Georges Braque

Wounded Birds

Colby Rodowsky

It's not that my mother doesn't understand, because she does. In fact, she understands so well, and so much, and so single-mindedly, that half the time she goes around with a glazed look in her eyes and forgets to get her hair cut, and go to the dentist and that we're almost out of toilet paper or tuna fish.

She makes her living understanding, which may make more sense when I tell you that my mother is Dr. Emma Hart. Now, if that doesn't help, then probably, like me until my consciousness was raised, you've always thought of radio as the place to hear the Top 40 or sometimes the weather report when you're heading for the shore on a summer Friday afternoon. But just try twiddling the dial and you'll find her, way over to the left on the band, next to the country and western station.

Maybe what I should do is go back a little and explain. You see, my mother is a psychotherapist, which means that she counsels people and tries to help them find ways of dealing with their problems. She's also a widow. My father died when I was a baby, and sometimes I try to imagine what it must have been like for her, taking care of a baby alone and trying to establish a practice all at the same time. One thing I'm sure of is that knowing Mom, she handled it gracefully, and stoically,[1] and with that funny way she has of biting her lower lip so that for all her hanging-in-there attitude she still looks like a ten-year-old kid—the kind you want to do something for because she's

---

1. **stoically** [stō′ ə kəl lē]: calmly and without showing feelings.

not always whining or sniffling. I guess you'd have to say that as much as possible my mother is in charge of her own life, which is the way she tries to get the people who call in to her on the radio to be.

The way the radio program got started was that several years ago the producer was looking for something to put on in the late afternoon when people were mostly fixing dinner or driving carpool or just sitting with their feet up. It wasn't exactly prime time. Then he remembered how he'd heard Mom speak at a dinner once and had thought at the time that putting someone like her on radio would be a real public service. Besides, the ratings couldn't be any lower than they had been for the Handy Home Fixit show he'd had on before. Anyway, he tracked her down, arranged for a test, and then Mom was on the air.

I never will forget that first show. I mean, there was my mother's voice coming out of our kitchen radio, sounding slightly frantic and giving those first callers more than they bargained for: I guess she was afraid if she let them off the line there wouldn't *be* any more. That day even the producer called with a question. And the boy in the studio who went for coffee. But Mom hung in there, and calls continued to come in, and then they started backing up, and it wasn't long before people opened by saying, "I didn't think I'd *ever* get through to you." After only a month on the air the Emma Hart show went from one hour to two; and the way I figured it, a lot of people were eating dinner later than they ever had before. Including us.

Mom really cared about the people who telephoned her, and almost right from the beginning she was calling them her "wounded birds." Not on the air, of course, and *never* to anyone but me. I got used to her looking up in the middle of dinner or from watching the late news on TV and saying, "I hope my wounded bird with the abusive husband will get herself into counseling" or "The wounded bird with those children who walk all over her had better learn to assert herself before it's too late." And *I* sure learned not to joke around: once I referred to one of her callers as a fractured canary and almost started World War III.

Not long after this, things really started to happen. First, Mom's show was moved to a better time slot. Then it was syndicated, so that she wasn't just on the air here but in a bunch of other cities, too. The way "Doonesbury" and "Dick Tracy" are in a bunch of newspapers. Now, I have to say that for the most part my mother's pretty cool about things, but the day she found out that the Emma Hart show was being syndicated she just about flipped. She called me from the studio and told me to meet her at the Terrace Garden for dinner, to be sure and get spiffed up because we were going all out.

During dinner Mom spent a lot of time staring into the candlelight and smiling to herself. Finally she said, "Just think of all those people who'll be listening now." And let me tell you, I *was* thinking about them, and it worried me a lot. I mean the way I saw it, there were going to be even more problems: more victims who were downtrodden or misunderstood. More stories about people who had been abused or who had kids on drugs or dropping out, or ne'er-do-well relatives moving in. But when I tried to say that, Mom was suddenly all attention. "Don't be silly, Amanda. It's the same amount of time and the same number of calls—you'll hardly notice any difference. Only now I'll have wounded birds in Phoenix and Pittsburgh and Philadelphia."

In one way she was right: the show sounded pretty much the same. (Except that *I* found out that when your husband/lover/friend walks out on you it hurts as much in Peoria[2] as it does in Perth Amboy.[3])

In another way she was wrong: she was busier than she had ever been before, what with traveling and lecturing and doing guest shows from other cities. For a while there, it was as if I was spending as much time at my best friend Terri's as I was at my own house. Then eventually Mom decided I could stay at our place when she had to be out of town, as long as Terri stayed there with me, which wasn't as good or as bad as it sounds, because Terri lives right across the street and her mother has X-ray eyes. I mean we can hardly manage to reach for our favorite breakfast of Twinkies and Oreo ice cream with an orange juice chaser before her mother is on the telephone telling us to eat cornflakes instead—and to wash the dishes.

2. **Peoria** [pē ôr′ ē ə]: city in central Illinois.
3. **Perth Amboy** [pėrth am boy]: a seaport in New Jersey.

Sometimes I felt that life was nothing but a revolving door: Mom going out while I was coming in. I know there are some kids who would've thought I was lucky, but the thing about my mother is that she's okay. And I wanted to see more of her. Besides that, I needed to talk to her. I don't know why, but all of a sudden it seemed that things were piling up around me. No major crises, you understand. Nothing that would exactly stop traffic.

I'll give you an example.

Take my friend Terri. I have a terrible feeling that she has a secret crush on my boyfriend Josh. If she does, it would be a disaster, because how could we really be friends anymore? But then again how could Terri and I *not* be friends? I'm not sure *why* I think this, unless it's because she gets quiet and acts bored when I talk about him a lot—the way you do when you don't want to let on about liking someone. I mean she couldn't *really* be bored. Could she?

Then there's Miss Spellman, my English teacher, who has this really atrocious breath and is forever leaning into people as she reads poetry in class. Imagine somebody breathing garbage fumes on you as she recites Emily Dickinson. If something doesn't happen soon I may never like poetry again.

Now, maybe these aren't world problems, any more than the incident with the guidance counselor was, but it bugged me all the same. Our school has an obsession about students getting into *good* colleges a.s.a.p.[4] and knowing what they want to do with the rest of their lives (Terri and I call it the life-packaging syndrome). Anyway, this particular day I was coming out of gym on my way to study hall when Mr. Burnside, the guidance counselor, stopped me and started asking me all this stuff, like what my career goals were and had I decided what I wanted to major in in college.

What I said (only politer than it sounds here) was that how did I know what I wanted to major in when I didn't even know where I wanted to *go* to college. Mr. Burnside got a wild look in his eyes and started opening and closing his mouth so that all I could see was a shiny strand of spit running between his top and bottom teeth while he

4. **a.s.a.p.:** abbreviation for "as soon as possible."

Central ceiling panel in the room of Henry II the Louvre, Georges Braque, Paris

lectured me on how I was going about this whole college thing the wrong way. He said I should come into the guidance office someday and let him feed me into the computer—well, not me exactly, but stuff like my grades, extra curricular activities, and whether or not I needed financial aid.

"And what does your mother say?" he asked as he rooted in his pocket for a late pass to get me into study hall. "You'll certainly have it easier than anybody else in your class, or the school either for that matter—living with Dr. Emma Hart." He laughed that horselaugh of his and slapped me on the back. "She'll get right to the *Hart* of it." Another laugh. "Anybody else'd have to call her on the telephone." His laughter seemed to follow me all the way to study hall. I even heard it bouncing around in my head as I settled down to do my Spanish.

"Anybody else'd have to call her on the telephone," he had said.

Why not? I thought as I was walking home from school. Why not? I asked myself when Josh and I were eating popcorn and playing Scrabble on the living room floor that night.

And pretty soon *why not?* changed to *when?* The answer to that one was easy though, because spring vacation was only a week and a half away and that would give me the perfect opportunity.

The funny thing was that once I'd decided to do it, I never worried about getting through. Maybe that was because I'd heard Mom say plenty of times that they always liked it when kids called into the show, and I guess I figured that unless everybody on spring vacation decided to call the Dr. Emma Hart Show, I wouldn't have any trouble. Besides, I practiced in the shower making my voice huskier than usual and just a little breathless, hoping that it would sound sincere and make an impression on Jordan, the guy who screens the calls and tries for just the right balance of men, women, and kids, with not too much emphasis on busted romances as opposed to anxiety attacks.

The next funny thing was that once I'd made up my mind to call Dr. Emma Hart, I began to feel like a wounded bird myself, and I was suddenly awfully glad that she cared about them the way she did. I had a little trouble deciding what I wanted to ask her on the show, and even before I could make up my mind I began to think of other things that bothered me too. Not problems, but stuff I'd like to talk over with Mom. Like Vietnam,[5] for example. I'd watched *Apocalypse Now*[6] on TV and there was a lot I didn't understand. And what about the sixties?—was Mom ever involved in sit-ins or walkouts or any of that? I somehow doubted it, but it would be important to know for sure. Finally it came to me: what I wanted to ask Dr. Hart about was not being able to talk to Mom because there she was all wrapped up with her wounded birds. Only the whole thing got confusing, one being the other and all.

Anyway, I did it. I put the call in just before eleven on the Monday morning of spring vacation and almost chickened out when Jordan answered. I had met him a couple of times down at the studio, and I could almost see him now, looking like some kind of an

5. **Vietnam** [vē et′ näm′]: country in Southeast Asia that was the scene of a war in which the United States was involved in the 1960s and 1970s.
6. *Apocalypse Now* [ə pok′ ə lips]: 1979 movie about the Vietnam War.

intense juggler who is trying to keep everything going at once. I heard my voice, as if it were coming from somewhere far away, giving my name as Claire (it's my middle name) and outlining my problem. When I got finished, Jordan said that he was putting me on hold and not to go away, that Dr. Hart would be with me shortly.

And all of a sudden she was. I mean, there I was talking to my own mother and telling her how I couldn't talk to my mother, and how the things I wanted to talk to her about weren't actually big deals anyway, but still—.

Dr. Hart let me go on for a while and then she broke in and said that it was important for me to know that my concerns were as real as anybody else's and it sounded as if my mother and I had a pretty good relationship that had just gotten a little off the track and what I had to do was be really up-front with her and let her know how I felt. Then she suggested that I make a date with my mother for lunch so that I could tell her (Mom) exactly what I'd told her (Dr. Emma Hart), and that I should be sure to call back and let her know how it worked out.

After that I said, "Okay," and "Thank you." Then I hung up.

The only trouble was that as soon as Mom got home that day I knew it wasn't going to work.

She was sort of coming unglued. It had been a bad day, she told me. One of her private patients was in the midst of a crisis; the producer of the show was having a fight with his wife and wanted to tell Mom all about it. She had a dinner speech to give Saturday night and didn't have a thought about what to say, and my uncle Alex had called from Scranton to ask Mom to try to talk some sense into his teenage son, who was driving them all crazy.

Then she looked at me and said, "Thank heavens you've got it all together."

Talk about guilt. Right away I knew I was going to break rule number one: I wasn't going to be able to be up-front.

The thing was, I knew I couldn't take what was already one rotten week for Mom and dump all my problems (which seemed to be getting bigger by the minute) on her. Even though I felt like I was going to explode.

By Friday I knew I needed another talk with Dr. Hart. After all, she'd said to call back, hadn't she?

Getting through Jordan was even easier the second time. All I had to say was that I'd spoken to Dr. Hart earlier in the week and that she'd said to let her know what happened.

"Oh, good, a success story," Jordan said right away, jumping to conclusions. I guess he knew what kind of a week it had been too. "Hold on; Dr. Hart will be with you soon," he said.

And there was Dr. Emma Hart again. And suddenly there *I* was, unloading about how what she had suggested wasn't going to work.

"Why not?" she wanted to know. "Did you try?"

"Yes—no," I said. Then I was going on again, all about Bad-Breath Spellman, the guidance counselor, and how maybe my best friend had a thing for my boyfriend. She kept steering me back to the subject of my mother and why I hadn't arranged to have lunch with her.

I said that my mother had had a bad week. That she was swamped, preoccupied, distracted, and running behind. And then it happened. I mean, I heard the words sliding off my lips and couldn't stop them. I said, "The thing about my mother is that she has all these wounded birds who have really important problems and they take all the time she has."

A silence ballooned up between us and was so loud I couldn't hear anything else—and if you know anything about radio, you know that the worst thing that can happen is silence. It lasted forever, and while it was going on I gave serious thought to running away from home, or at least hanging up.

When Mom finally spoke, her voice sounded choked, as if she had swallowed a gumball.

"We've been talking to Claire this morning, who is really Amanda," she said. "And one of the things we talk a lot about on this show is saying what you have to say—even if that's not always easy. Are you still there, Amanda?"

"Yes," I squeaked.

"If I know Amanda," my mother went on, "she would rather have run away, or hung up, but instead she did something harder. She hung on."

I gulped.

"Amanda is my daughter, and it seems we have some things to talk about, so what I'm going to do is to ask my assistant to make a reservation for lunch at the Terrace Garden." Then it sounded as though Mom had moved in closer to the microphone and was speaking just to me. "If you hurry, Amanda, I'll meet you at 1:30. So we can talk."

And we did: about Bad-Breath Spellman, and Terri, and how it's okay not to know now what I want to do with the rest of my life.

We talked about saving the whales, and our two weeks at the shore this summer, and how some day we're going to Ireland. About books and movies and the time in fourth grade when I got the chicken pox and Mom caught them from me.

And we talked about how we had missed talking to each other and what we could do about it.

We ate lunch slowly, and took ages deciding on dessert, and ages more eating it.

We sat there all afternoon, until the light streaking in the windows changed from yellow to a deep, burning gold and the busboys started setting the tables for dinner.

COLBY RODOWSKY

Colby Rodowsky was born in Baltimore, Maryland. She lived in New York City and later in Washington, D.C., where she taught grade school. She later returned to Baltimore with her family.

Rodowsky's books are about teenagers who find themselves in serious situations. Some situations, such as the one in Rodowsky's book *P.S. Write Soon*, are the result of the character's choices or actions. Other situations, like the one in *A Summer's Worth of Shame*, are caused by forces beyond the character's control. Rodowsky's characters, such as Amanda in "Amanda and the Wounded Birds," have to work things out for themselves.

DANIELLE O'MARA

MEL GLENN

When my parents went away on a short vacation,
I stayed with my older sister, Madeline,
Who works for a real estate office downtown.
I simmered while she nagged me to
Wash the dishes, do the laundry, finish my homework.   5
Nothing I did was good enough for her.
Many evenings ended in heated arguments and slammed doors.
When she told me she was bringing a date home,
I decided to surprise her by making dinner.
I used the cookbook but,   10
The fish was raw,
The spaghetti limp,
The biscuits burnt,
And the poor guy staggered out the door, holding his stomach.
I thought my sister would fry me.   15
She looked at me and said,
"I didn't like him anyway."
We burst out giggling and hugged each other.

MEL GLENN

Mel Glenn was born in 1943 in Switzerland, but grew up in New York City. After college, Glenn became a journalist. During the 1960s, as a Peace Corps volunteer, he taught in West Africa, and continued teaching after he returned home.

Glenn's poetry and novels are based on his classroom experiences. "I write about what I know," he says. The basic idea for his first book, *Class Dismissed,* came from Edgar Lee Masters' *Spoon River Anthology,* in which people tell their own stories. "Danielle O'Mara" is from *Class Dismissed II: More High School Poems.*

A Game of

Richard Wilbur

Catch

Monk and Glennie were playing catch on the side lawn of the firehouse when Scho caught sight of them. They were good at it, for seventh-graders, as anyone could see right away. Monk, wearing a catcher's mitt, would lean easily sidewise and back, with one leg lifted and his throwing hand almost down to the grass, and then lob the white ball straight up into the sunlight. Glennie would shield his eyes with his left hand and, just as the ball fell past him, snag it with a little dart of his glove. Then he would burn the ball straight toward Monk, and it would spank into the round mitt and sit, like a still-life apple on a plate, until Monk flipped it over into his right hand and, with a negligent flick of his hanging arm, gave Glennie a fast grounder.

They were going on and on like that, in a kind of slow, mannered, luxurious dance in the sun, their faces perfectly blank and entranced, when Glennie noticed Scho dawdling along the other side of the street and called hello to him. Scho crossed over and stood at the front edge of the lawn, near an apple tree, watching.

"Got your glove?" asked Glennie after a time. Scho obviously hadn't.

"You could give me some easy grounders," said Scho.

"But don't burn 'em."

"All right," Glennie said. He moved off a little, so the three of them formed a triangle, and they passed the

ball around for about five minutes, Monk tossing easy grounders to Scho, Scho throwing to Glennie, and Glennie burning them in to Monk. After a while, Monk began to throw them back to Glennie once or twice before he let Scho have his grounder, and finally Monk gave Scho a fast, bumpy grounder that hopped over his shoulder and went into the brake on the other side of the street.

"Not so hard," called Scho as he ran across to get it.

"You should've had it," Monk shouted.

It took Scho a little while to find the ball among the ferns and dead leaves, and when he saw it, he grabbed it up and threw it toward Glennie. It struck the trunk of the apple tree, bounced back at an angle, and rolled steadily and stupidly onto the cement apron in front of the firehouse, where one of the trucks was parked. Scho ran hard and stopped it just before it rolled under the truck, and this time he carried it back to his former position on the lawn and threw it carefully to Glennie.

"I got an idea," said Glennie. "Why don't Monk and I catch for five minutes more, and then you can borrow one of our gloves?"

"That's all right with me," said Monk. He socked his fist into his mitt, and Glennie burned one in.

"All right," Scho said, and went over and sat under the tree. There in the shade he watched them resume their skillful play. They threw lazily fast or lazily slow— high, low, or wide—and always handsomely, their expressions serene,[1] changeless, and forgetful. When Monk missed a low backhand catch, he walked indolently[2] after the ball and, hardly even looking, flung it sidearm for an imaginary put-out.[3] After a good while of this, Scho said, "Isn't it five minutes yet?"

"One minute to go," said Monk, with a fraction of a grin.

Scho stood up and watched the ball slap back and forth for several minutes more, and then he turned and pulled himself up into the crotch of the tree.

1. **serene** [sə rēn′]: calm, peaceful.
2. **indolently** [in′ dl ənt lē]: lazily, idly.
3. **put-out** [pùt′ out′]: an action that puts the batter or base runner out of the game.

"Where you going?" Monk asked.

"Just up the tree," Scho said.

"I guess he doesn't want to catch," said Monk.

Scho went up and up through the fat light-gray branches until they grew slender and bright and gave under him. He found a place where several supple branches were knit to make a dangerous chair, and sat there with his head coming out of the leaves into the sunlight. He could see the two other boys down below, the ball going back and forth between them as if they were bowling on the grass, and Glennie's crew-cut head looking like a sea urchin.[4]

"I found a wonderful seat up here," Scho said loudly. "If I don't fall out." Monk and Glennie didn't look up or comment, and so he began jouncing gently in his chair of branches and singing "Yo-ho, heave ho" in an exaggerated way.

"Do you know what, Monk?" he announced in a few moments. "I can make you two guys do anything I want. Catch that ball, Monk! Now you catch it, Glennie!"

"I was going to catch it anyway," Monk suddenly said. "You're not making anybody do anything when they're already going to do it anyway."

"I made you say what you just said," Scho replied joyfully.

"No, you didn't," said Monk, still throwing and catching but now less serenely absorbed in the game.

"That's what I wanted you to say," Scho said.

The ball bounced off the rim of Monk's mitt and plowed into a gladiolus[5] bed beside the firehouse, and Monk ran to get it while Scho jounced in his treetop and sang, "I wanted you to miss that. Anything you do is what I wanted you to do."

"Let's quit for a minute," Glennie suggested.

"We might as well, until the peanut gallery[6] shuts up," Monk said.

---

4. **sea urchin:** a small, round sea animal with a spiny shell.

5. **gladiolus** [glad′ ē ō′ ləs]: a plant with sword-shaped leaves and spikes of large flowers in various colors.

6. **peanut gallery:** slang for people offering uninvited, insignificant comments or advice.

They went over and sat cross-legged in the shade of the tree. Scho looked down between his legs and saw them on the dim spotty ground, saying nothing to one another. Glennie soon began abstractedly spinning his glove between his palms; Monk pulled his nose and stared out across the lawn.

"I want you to mess around with your nose, Monk," said Scho, giggling. Monk withdrew his hand from his face.

"Do that with your glove, Glennie," Scho persisted. "Monk, I want you to pull up hunks of grass and chew on it."

Glennie looked up and saw a self-delighted, intense face staring down at him through the leaves. "Stop being a dope and come down and we'll catch for a few minutes," he said.

Scho hesitated, and then said, in a tentatively[7] mocking voice, "That's what I wanted you to say."

"All right, then, nuts to you," said Glennie.

"Why don't you keep quiet and stop bothering people?" Monk asked.

"I made you say that," Scho replied, softly.

"Shut up," Monk said.

"I made you say that, and I want you to be standing there looking sore. And I want you to climb up the tree! I'm making you do it!"

Monk was scrambling up through the branches, awkward in his haste, and getting snagged on twigs. His face was furious and foolish, and he kept telling Scho to shut up, shut up, shut up, while the other's exuberant[8] and panicky voice poured down upon his head.

"*Now* you shut up or you'll be sorry," Monk said, breathing hard as he reached up and threatened to shake the cradle of slight branches in which Scho was sitting.

"I *want*—" Scho screamed as he fell. Two lower branches broke his rustling, crackling fall, but he landed on his back with a deep thud and lay still, with a strangled look on his face and his eyes clenched. Glennie knelt down and asked breathlessly, "Are you

7. **tentatively** [ten′ tə tiv lē]: carefully, hesitatingly.
8. **exuberant** [eg zü′ bər ənt]: in high spirits, happy.

O.K., Scho? Are you O.K.?," while Monk swung down through the leaves crying that honestly he hadn't even touched him, the crazy guy just let go. Scho doubled up and turned over on his right side, and now both the other boys knelt beside him, pawing at his shoulder and begging to know how he was.

Then Scho rolled away from them and sat partly up, still struggling to get his wind but forcing a species[9] of smile onto his face.

"I'm sorry, Scho," Monk said. "I didn't mean to make you fall."

Scho's voice came out weak and gravelly, in gasps. "I meant—you to do it. You—had to. You can't do—anything—unless I want—you to."

Glennie and Monk looked helplessly at him as he sat there, breathing a bit more easily and smiling fixedly, with tears in his eyes. Then they picked up their gloves and the ball, walked over to the street, and went slowly away down the sidewalk, Monk punching his fist into the mitt, Glennie juggling the ball between glove and hand.

From under the apple tree, Scho, still bent over a little for lack of breath, croaked after them in triumph and misery, "I want you to do whatever you're going to do for the whole rest of your life!"

9. **species** [spē′ shēz]: kind, type.

R I C H A R D   W I L B U R
....

Richard Wilbur was born in 1921 and grew up in rural New England. He is best known as a poet whose poems often focus on nature. These subjects, Wilbur says, come from a childhood full of woods and cornfields, horses and haywagons. Two of his poetry collections are *Things of This World* and *The Beautiful Changes*.

Among his other achievements, Wilbur has become an expert on the life and works of the nineteenth-century American author, Edgar Allan Poe.

UMU MADU *in the* GOOD OLD DAYS

T. OBINKARAM ECHEWA

There was once a village called Umu Madu[1] where the people loved to have feasts. Every chance the villagers had, they called a feast to celebrate one thing or another.

"There is a new moon in the sky," the people of Umu Madu would say sometimes. "Let us have a feast to celebrate it."

"The moon is now full," the villagers might say a few weeks later. "Let us have a feast to celebrate the full moon."

At the beginning of the farming season, after they had planted their crops, the people of Umu Madu had a feast.

In the middle of the farming season, after the rains had started and the farms were green with growing crops, the people of Umu Madu held a feast.

At the end of the farming season, after the crops had been harvested and placed in the barns, the people of Umu Madu had a feast.

Sometimes even when nothing happened, the people of Umu Madu had a feast. If anyone asked them what the feast was for, they replied: "We are having this feast because nothing has happened."

Some of the feasts were small and some were big, but always there was a feast in the village of Umu Madu, and all the feasts were long and happy.

All the feasts were held under the big cottonwood tree in the middle of the market clearing at the center of the village of Umu Madu. The men killed the chickens or the goats or a cow, depending on how big the feast was. They also cut up the meat and cooked it in

1. **Umu Madu** [ü′ mü mä′ dü]

Raffia cloth Shoowa people, Kasai river area, Zaire, c. 1935, Museum of New Mexico

big iron pots, which they stirred with long sticks. The women cooked the soup and the stew as well as the rice and the fufu.[2] Children fetched water or firewood and darted here and there on errands for the adults.

When everything was ready, the elders of Umu Madu appointed four or five young men to divide the food so that every man, woman and child would get a share. Fufu and rice were piled high on everyone's plate. Big pieces of meat stuck out above the surface of everyone's stew and soup. However, the heart of the feast was the big lumps of meat which were spread out in long rows on banana leaves or raffia mats. From the oldest man to the youngest child, the people of Umu Madu chose their shares of meat according to their ages.

For as long as anyone could remember, the people of Umu Madu had always eaten their feasts on the ground. Some people squatted onto the ground. Some people knelt on the ground. Some people sat on the ground.

2. **fufu** [fü fü′]: dish comprised of bananas, squash, or yams.

Then one day a stranger arrived in the village of Umu Madu.

This was not the first time a stranger had come to Umu Madu. However, this stranger was very strange. No one had ever seen or heard anyone like him before. The villagers nicknamed the stranger No Skin because his skin had no color. No Skin had hair which looked like corn silk and eyes which shone like glass beads. At first everyone thought he had no toes, until he took off his shoes and allowed some of the villagers to count his toes. He had ten of them.

"Urupirisi. Urupirisi. Urupirisi," No Skin said to the villagers of Umu Madu. When someone was found who could understand No Skin's language, what he was saying was: "What have we here? Why are intelligent people like you eating their feast on the ground?"

"We have always eaten our feasts on the ground," the villagers replied. "Where do you want us to eat? On the treetops or in the sky?"

"Haven't you ever heard of tables?" No Skin asked.

"No," the villagers replied, surprised and a little ashamed. "We have never heard of tables. What are tables?"

No Skin began describing a table to the people of Umu Madu. He drew a picture of a table on the ground for them as he said: "My friends, these are modern times. If you want to be modern and up to date, you must stop eating on the ground and start eating on tables."

"Where can we find a table?" the villagers begged. "We do not want to be left behind by progress. We want to be modern and up to date."

"No problem," No Skin replied. "Send along four ablebodied men with me, and they will bring back a table to the village within a week."

Within a week, just as No Skin had promised, there was a table in the village of Umu Madu. It was big and long and heavy, and the villagers spent many hours admiring it, walking around it, rubbing their hands on it, and smiling at their reflections on its shiny top.

"This table is so good," the elders of the village said, "that we cannot wait until the next feast several weeks from now to try it. Let us have a feast at once and try the new table."

Everyone thought that was a good idea.

So a feast was called immediately. Two cows were killed. Fufu and rice were cooked in abundance. Everyone in the village came out to enjoy the big feast on the new table. No one bothered about raffia mats and banana leaves anymore.

However, as the young men who had been appointed by the elders began to divide the meat, they made a disturbing discovery. There was not enough space around the table for everyone.

"We have a problem here," one old man said. "How are we going to solve it?"

"Why don't the elders go into a conference with one another, as is our custom," someone suggested. "Let the elders tell us what to do about this problem."

"Yes, yes," everyone agreed. "Let the elders decide for us."

So the elders went into a conference. After a long time, they came back to the assembly and announced: "We cannot agree on how to satisfy everyone about the table. We cannot agree who should eat at the table and who should not. So we have decided instead to return the table to No Skin, so we can continue our unity and eat our feasts on the ground together, as we have always done. If we cannot find No Skin, we can put the table away, and he can take it back whenever he comes this way again."

"No-o-o-oh!" many members of the assembly shouted. There was a lot of murmuring and grumbling.

Then one young man said: "We now have the table, and everyone agrees it is a good thing. Would it not be foolish to let it sit idle? Would it not be even more foolish to give it back to No Skin? . . . All members of the assembly of Umu Madu who agree with me, please say Hay-ay-ay!"

"Hay-ay-ay!" everyone in the assembly seemed to shout.

The elders were surprised and disappointed. Not often did the community assembly fail to heed their advice. "All right," the elders said, "if that is the will of Umu Madu, then so be it. However, we will choose positions around the table according to age. Old people will choose first. People of Umu Madu, show that you agree with us by saying Hay-ay-ay!"

"Hay-ay-ay!" most voices shouted.

However, there were some voices which said "No!"

The village of Umu Madu liked to do things by having everyone agree. So the elders said, "If we cannot do it by age, how then shall we do it?"

One young man raised his hand and was given permission to speak.

"The times we live in are modern times," the young man said. "Modern times and modern things like the table are for the young. So I say, the young men should eat at the table. The elders can eat on the ground. Everyone who agrees with me say Hay-ay-ay!"

"Hay-ay-ay!" most of the young people shouted.

"No-o-o-oh!" most of the older people shouted.

The village of Umu Madu was faced with one of the sharpest disagreements its community assembly had ever seen. The elders looked at one another, shook their heads and scratched them. Then one elder cleared his throat and said:

"Perhaps we can do it by volunteering. Perhaps some people will volunteer to eat on the ground."

Everyone thought that was a good idea. However, when the elder said, "Who will volunteer to eat on the ground?" people began to answer: "Someone else."

"Who else?" the elders asked.

"Anyone else but me," everyone said.

At this point the elders decided to go into another conference. For a long time and after many debates they still could not agree on what to do. In the end they decided to settle the matter by drawing sticks. Anyone who drew a short stick would eat on the ground. Anyone who drew a long stick would eat at the table.

However, by the time the elders returned from their conference to announce their decision, the people were pushing, shoving, and fighting for places around the table.

"Shame!" the elders cried in dismay. "Shame, Umu Madu, shame!"

When the fighting stopped, the elders said, "All right, all right, if this is what we have been driven to, then let everyone keep the place he now has. Those of you who have occupied places around the table, keep your places. Those of you who are on the ground, stay on the ground. But please stop fighting like hyenas. We came here to feast, not to fight."

That was how the matter was settled for that day. However, it did not end there. Disunity had come to the feasts of Umu Madu, because when there was a feast some people ate at the table and some people on the ground. Envy had come to the feasts of Umu Madu. Those who ate on the ground looked enviously or rolled their eyes at those who ate at the table. Pride had come to the feasts of Umu Madu. Those who ate at the table stuck up their noses in the air and looked down on those who ate on the ground. Unhappiness had come to the feasts of Umu Madu. For the first time ever, everyone was not happy at the feasts.

Every feast that the people of Umu Madu held now ended in a fight. People came to the feasts not just to enjoy themselves but to fight for places around the table. Those who had eaten on the ground during the last feast thought it was their turn to eat at the table this time. However, those who had eaten at the table the last time thought they should do so again.

"Once a person has fought to get a place by the table," some of the villagers said, "he should keep it permanently."

Some villagers even felt that once a person had begun to eat at the table, his wives and children should also eat at the table, and even his children and his children's children, whenever they were born, should have the future right to eat at the table.

Some villagers became so angry at what was going on that they refused to attend any more feasts.

Then one day just before a very big feast, someone secretly sawed more than halfway through one of the table's legs. In the middle of the feast, when the meat and all other goodies had been heaped on the table, the leg broke, the table tipped over, and all the meat fell to the ground.

Various people accused one another of the trick. A big free-for-all fight broke out. Pots were broken. Basins of rice were kicked over. The meat was trampled underfoot.

The day after the big fight, the elders called everyone together in the market clearing. "Umu Madu," the elders said, "the table which No Skin gave us has been nothing but trouble. There is only one way to solve our problem—destroy the table before it destroys us."

"Hay-ay-ay!" the whole assembly responded in unison. "Let us destroy the table before it destroys us!"

The men, women, and children of Umu Madu went home and got their axes, machetes,[3] clubs, and pestles[4] and set upon the table and smashed it to pieces.

"Now we can be one again," one elder said after the task was done.

"Yes," another elder replied. "We can eat our feasts in unity and harmony once again."

"Yes," someone else in the assembly said. "Let us call a feast immediately to celebrate our freedom from the table."

"Yes, yes," everyone agreed.

A date was set for the special feast. Three cows were killed. Banana leaves and clean raffia mats were laid out on the swept ground, as in the old days. This was going to be the biggest and happiest feast Umu Madu had ever had.

However, just as the feast was about to start, someone pointed out that a few villagers had brought their own little, private tables to the feast.

"Why?" the elders asked. "Did we not agree to eat together on the ground as we used to do before No Skin brought us the table?"

"We agreed! Yes, we agreed!" a majority of the assembly replied.

"Why then have some people brought tables?" the elders asked.

3. **machetes** [mə shetʹ ēs]: large, heavy knives used for cutting brush.
4. **pestles** [pesʹ əlz]: club-shaped tools for pounding substances into powder.

"I now like tables," one table owner said. "I found No Skin, and he said I can have my own table if I wish. So, since I enjoy eating at a table, why shouldn't I be able to do so?"

"Me, too," another table owner said. "I not only like tables, but I have become so used to them that I can no longer bear to eat my meals on the ground."

Other table owners gave similar answers.

"You must destroy the tables," the elders commanded, "so that we can have harmony and unity as of old."

"My table is mine to do with as I please," one table owner said in an insulting voice. "It cost me plenty of money. No one can destroy it."

Another table owner agreed with the first one. He said: "If I cannot eat *my* part of the feast on *my* table, then I will not share in the feast at all!"

So the big feast which was supposed to bring back peace and harmony to Umu Madu instead brought disharmony and discord. There was first a long argument and then a big fight, during which many bones were broken. Since that day harmony and unity left the village and have not returned.

T. OBINKARAM ECHEWA

T. Obinkaram Echewa was born in 1940 in Nigeria, Africa. Echewa came to the United States when he was 21. He graduated from the University of Notre Dame and went on to Columbia University and the University of Pennsylvania.

While doing graduate work, Echewa not only taught English but wrote his first book—a novel. "I have been side-stepping along in my career looking for an outlet," Echewa said at that time. "Perhaps I will find it in writing serious fiction." Since then, Echewa has rediscovered the value of tales and humorous anecdotes from "the good old days" in his home country.

THE CLEARING

Night Firing of Tobacco Thomas Hart Benton, 194_
oil and tempera on canvas, 20" x 31", United Missou_
Bank, Kansas City

JESSE STUART

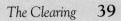

Finn and I were pruning the plum trees around our garden when a rock came cracking among the branches of the tree I was pruning.

"Where did that come from?" I asked Finn, who was on the ground below piling the branches.

"I don't know," he said.

Then we heard the Hinton boys laughing on the other side of the valley. I went back to pruning. In less than a minute, a rock hit the limb above my head and another rock hit at Finn's feet. Then I came down from the tree. Finn and I started throwing rocks. In a few minutes rocks were falling like hailstones around them and around us. The land was rocky on both sides of the valley and there were plenty of rocks to throw.

One of their rocks hit Finn on the foot and one of our rocks peeled the largest Hinton boy's head.

"Think of it," Finn said. "We fight before we know each other's names! What will it be as time goes on?"

We fought all afternoon with rocks. At sunset the Hinton boys took off up the path and over the hill. We went home. When Pa asked why we hadn't finished pruning the trees, we told him.

"I told you," he said to Mom. "You'll see whether we can live apart or not."

"Wait until we know them and they know us," Mom said.

"But how are we ever goin' to know people like them?" Pa asked.

"Oh, something will happen," she replied calmly. "You'll see."

Next day Mort Hinton was with his boys. They climbed higher on the hill, cutting the briers[1] and brush and tree laps and stacking them neatly into piles. Finn and I pruned our trees.

---

1. **briers** [brī ̆ ərz]: bushes that have prickly stems, such as the blackberry plant or wild rose.

"I'll say one thing for the Hintons," Mom said. "They're good workers."

"When they don't throw rocks," Finn said.

My guineas[2] flew across the valley where the Hintons were clearing land, on the fourth day.

"Get these back on your side the valley," Mort Hinton yelled. "Get 'em back where they belong."

I didn't want to put my guineas in the henhouse. But I had to. I knew Mort Hinton would kill them. I wanted to tell him that they would help his land. They'd rid it of insects that might destroy his crop. Buit I was afraid to tell him anything.

A week had passed before my guineas got out and flew across the valley.

"If you don't keep your guineas on your side of the valley," Morton Hinton hollered to me, "I'll wring their infernal necks."

That night I put my guineas up again. I fixed the henhouse so they couldn't get out and roam the hills as they had always done. While Finn, Pa and I cleared land on one side of the valley, the Hintons cleared on the other side.

Though we'd never been close enough to the Hintons to talk with them and we didn't want to get that close, we found ourselves trying to do more work than the four of them. Each day, that early March, rain or sunshine, four Hintons worked on their side of the valley, and Pa, Finn and I worked on our side. One day a Hinton boy hollered at us, "You can't clear as much land as we can."

"Don't answer him," Pa said.

The next day Mrs. Hinton came to the clearing and worked with them. Mom watched her using a sprouting hoe, a mattock,[3] brier scythe[4] and an ax.

"She works like a man," Mom said, as she watched her from the window. "Poor woman. I feel sorry for her. Out working like that!"

2. **guineas** [gin′ ēz]: large, dark, speckled birds, similar to pheasants, which are often raised for food.
3. **mattock** [mat′ ək]: a large tool with a steel head and a flat blade, used for loosening soil and cutting roots.
4. **scythe** [sīth]: a long, curved blade on a long handle used for cutting grass.

"Other women work," Pa snapped. "You work, don't you?"

"When I'm pregnant, I don't get out in the cold March wind and clear ground," Mom said.

"I didn't know she was pregnant," Pa said.

"Well, she is," Mom answered.

When April came and the Hintons had finished clearing the hill, and had burned the brush, Mort Hinton brought a skinny mule hitched to a cutter plow and started plowing the newground. He plowed slowly the first day. The second day my guineas got out again and flew across the valley to the plowed ground. Mort Hinton caught two of them, twisted their necks and threw them down into the valley. The others flew back home when he tried to catch them. Then he yelled across to where we were plowing our newground and told us what he had done.

"I feel like taking a shotgun and sprinkling him," I said.

"Your guineas were on his land," Mom said. "He'd told you to put them up."

Mort Hinton plowed his newground by working from daylight until dusk, while Mrs. Hinton and the boys carried armloads of roots from the field and stacked them in great heaps. By the first of May they had made this rooty newground soil like a garden. Then came a rainy season in early May and they carried baskets of tobacco plants and set them in the straight-furrowed[5] rows.

"They're workers, all right," Pa said, agreeing with Mom. "But I don't understand how a man can let his wife get out there and drop tobacco plants when she is so near to being a mother again."

"Maybe they have to work to live," Mom said.

"Not like that," Pa said.

On a dark night about a week later I watched from my upstairs window a moving light. It came from the direction of Hintons', over the hill and down into the valley below our house. In a few minutes I heard footsteps on the porch. Then a loud knock on our door. I heard Pa get out of bed and open the door.

5. **straight-furrowed** [fėr′ ōd]: cut in long, narrow grooves by a plow.

Detail from **Night Firing of Tobacco**,
Thomas Hart Benton

The Clearing   41

"I'm Mort Hinton," a voice said. "My wife sent for your wife."

I heard Mom getting out of bed.

"I'll be ready in a minute," she called out.

Neither Pa nor Mort said another word.

"I'll be back when everything is all right," Mom told Pa as she hurried away.

I watched the lantern fade from sight as Mort Hinton and Mom went down the path into the deep valley below the house. In two minutes or more it flashed into sight again when they reached Hinton's tobacco field. The light moved swiftly up and over the hill. Next morning Pa cooked breakfast for us. He quarreled about Hintons as he stood near the hot stove frying eggs.

"Yeah, when they need something over there," Pa grumbled and muttered.

"Dollie Hinton's got a pretty girl baby over there," were Mom's first words as she sat down for a cup of coffee.

"What did they name the baby?" Glenna asked.

"They've not named her yet," Mom said. "Think they plan to call her Ethel. They're tickled to death. Six boys and now a girl!"

"What kind of people are they, anyway?" Pa asked.

"Like other people," Mom said. "They don't have much furniture in their house. They're working hard to pay for their farm."

"Will they be any better neighbors?" Pa asked.

"I think so," Mom said. "That hill over there is not a fence between us any longer."

"There's more than a hill between us," I said. "What about my guineas Mort Hinton killed? Did he say anything about 'em last night?"

"And what about the Hinton boy that hit me on the foot with a rock?" Finn said. "I'd like to meet up with him sometime."

By the time we had finished our breakfast, Mort Hinton was plowing the young tobacco. His three sons were hoeing the tender plants with long-handled gooseneck hoes.

"Looks like Mr. Hinton would be sleepy," Mom said. "He never went to bed last night. And the boys slept on the hay in the barn loft."

Pa, Finn and I didn't have too much sympathy for the Hintons. Through the dining-room window we could look across the valley and watch Mort keep the plow moving steadily. We watched his boys dig with their hoes, never looking up from the ground.

"This will be a dry, sunny day," Pa said. "We'll burn the brush piles on the rest of our clearing."

We gathered our pitchforks, hoes and rakes and went to the hill where we had cleared ground all spring. There were hundreds of brush piles on our twenty acres of cleared ground. The wind was still. The sun had dried the dew from the leaves and tufts of broom sage that carpeted the ground between the brush piles.

"It's the right time to burn," Pa said, holding up his hand. "I can't feel any wind. The brush has seasoned in these piles until it is as dry as powder."

Pa struck a match to the brush pile at the bottom of the clearing. The fire started with

Detail from **Night Firing of Tobacco**, Thomas Hart Benton

little leaps over the leaf-carpeted ground. Finn, Pa and I fired along the bottom of the clearing until we had a continuous line of fire going up the slope. Then a wind sprang from nowhere. And when flames leaped from brush pile to brush pile, Pa looked at me.

"This is out of control," Pa said. "Grab a hoe and start raking a ring."

"I'm afraid we can't stop it," Finn said. "We'll have to work fast if we save the orchards."

"Shut up and run to the house and get Sall and Glenna," Pa yelled.

"Look, Pa," Finn said, pointing down the hill.

Mort Hinton was in front. He was running up the hill. His three sons were running behind him, each with a hoe across his shoulder.

"It's out of control," Pa shouted to Mort before he reached us.

"We've come to help," Mort said.

"Can we keep it from the orchards?" Pa asked.

"Let's run to the top of the hill and fire against it," Mort said. "I've burnt hundreds of acres of clearing on hillsides and I always fire the top first and let it burn down! I fire the bottom last. Maybe we'll not be too late to save the orchards!"

Mort ran up the hill and we followed. Finn and I didn't speak to his boys and they didn't speak to us. But when we started raking a ring side by side, we started talking to the Hintons. We forgot about the rock fight. Now wasn't the time to remember it, when flames down under the hill were shooting twenty to thirty feet high. In no time we raked the ring across the top of the clearing. And the fire Mort Hinton set along the ring burned fiercely down the hill and made the ring wider and wider. Only once fire blew across the ring, and Pa stopped it then.

As soon as we had this spot under control, we raked a ring down the west side near the peach orchard. Mort set a line of fire along this ring and let it burn toward the middle of the clearing. Then we raked a ring on the east side and fired against the fire that was approaching our plum trees and our house. Soon the leaping flames met in the clearing. We had the fire under control. Our clearing was burned clean as a whistle.

"How much do I owe you?" Pa asked Mort Hinton.

"You don't owe me anything, Mick," Mort said. "We're just paying you back for the help your wife gave us last night."

"Then let's go to the house for dinner," Pa said.

"Some other time," Mort said. "We must go home and see about Dollie and the baby."

As we went down the hill, Finn and I talked with Big Adger, Al and Little Mort about squirrel hunting and wild-bee trees, while Pa and Mort laughed and talked about weather and crops.

JESSE STUART

Jesse Stuart [1906-1984] was born in a one-room log cabin in Greenup County, Kentucky, so far in the hills that he was fifteen before he saw an electric light or a telephone. Stuart often had to leave school to help support the family. Because he had missed so much elementary school, high school was a struggle. He succeeded because he loved to read.

Stuart worked his way through college and began teaching school in his home county, writing in his spare time. During the 1960s, he worked as a lecturer for the U.S. Information Service, traveling all over the world. Eventually he published more than fifty books—fiction, nonfiction, and poetry—nearly all to do with Appalachian country life. One of his best known books, *The Thread That Runs So True*, tells of his years teaching in Greenup County.

The Long Way Around

JEAN McCORD

I hadn't spoken to my stepmother in three days. I was absorbed by an inner grief and anger because she had given away my mother's dresses to the Salvation Army.

I could still feel my mother around the house. Sometimes I'd come bursting in from school with some important piece of news that I wanted to share immediately, and coming through the door, I'd shout, "Mother, I'm home. Where are you?" and instantly, before the echo had died, I'd remember, too late.

My stepmother had answered once, the first time, coming out from her bedroom with a smile on her face, thinking I was calling her, saying "Yes, Patty, what is it?" But my face was set in a frozen scowl, and I was standing there rigid, unyielding and furious at myself for such a mistake. She understood and turning away without pressing me any further, she went back into her room and closed her door.

My mother had died two years before when I was twelve, and even though I knew better, sometimes in the middle of the night, I'd awake in a terrible fear and to comfort myself back to sleep I'd whisper into the pillow, "She's only gone away on a trip. And she'll be back." In the morning I had to face my own lie.

My father had married again last year and though my two little brothers, Jason and Scott, called this new woman "Mother," my father had told me I didn't have to do so. I called her Alice even though sometimes it felt strange to call a grown woman by her first name. This Alice wasn't anything at all like my own mother. For one thing, she couldn't cook. My mother had been the best cook in the whole neighborhood. Even the other mothers around us used to say that and would come over for coffee and butter scones and things that my mother would just whip up on a moment's notice. This Alice . . . well, sometimes our whole supper ended up in the garbage can, and my father would take us out to a restaurant. I thought it was pretty stupid and expensive, but of course Jason and Scott loved it.

To make things even worse, so it seemed to me, my father had taken a new job, and we had moved away from the town and the neighborhood where I'd spent my whole life with kids I knew and had grown up with and gone to school with and graduated with.

Now I was in Jr. High with a whole new batch of kids and I didn't like any of them. They didn't like me, either. I kept my distance and when school was over, I walked home alone, carrying my books with my head down and hurrying by the groups of girls laughing and giggling over some private joke. I could feel them looking at my back and the talk always hushed a little until I was by, then they'd break out into silly, stifled snickers when I was down the street aways.

Actually I hated them all. I hated the teachers and the new school and my new stepmother and my father who seemed a new person too. Even my little brothers seemed to deserve a good slap for the way they had forgotten and called this Alice "Mother" as if they had never had a mother of their own.

The only one who hadn't changed, who was still the way he had always been, was Rufus, our old Samoyed.[1] Rufus is as old as I am, and

1. **Samoyed** [sam′ ə yəd′]: a Russian breed of medium-sized husky dogs that have long, thick, white fur.

in his way he understood. After my mother died, he'd lain on his braided rag rug and refused to move for over two weeks. He wouldn't eat because he was used to my mother fixing him up a strange mixture of dog food with raw egg and bacon drippings, and nobody else seemed to know just how to do it. Finally I tried and after a while he ate while looking at me from the corner of his eyes and seeming to apologize for it. I sat down beside him and cried into his neck, and he stopped eating long enough to lick my face which only made me cry harder.

Now the only reason I had for getting up in the morning was to greet Rufus and give him an egg. After school the only reason I came home was to take Rufus for a walk and together we had covered most of this new town. The only trouble was that the town stayed new. Somehow no matter how often we walked down the same streets, the houses always seemed strange. Rufus would plod along at my side, his head just at the reach of my hand. He stumbled once in a while over a curb, but that was because his eyesight wasn't too good any more. My own eyesight seemed slightly affected too because there was a gray film between me and everything I looked at.

We walked all over town after school, my feet just leading the two of us. Finally I knew we had tromped over every square inch of all the streets, but still nothing looked familiar. Sometimes returning home, I woudn't even know we had reached the end of the walk until Rufus turned off the sidewalk and went up our front steps.

One Saturday morning I woke up very early. This was about a month ago, I think, or maybe two months. I had lain awake a long time that night watching the shadow patterns change on the ceiling when the wind tossed the big snowball bush outside my window. It seemed like the night was trying to tell me something, but I couldn't quite make out what it was. Out in the kitchen I could hear that Rufus was awake, too, because every time he left his rug and walked across the floor, his toenails clicked on the linoleum. He seemed to be pacing the floor as if he wanted to go out into the night. Maybe he sensed something waiting out there for him. If my mother had been here, she'd know . . . she would have known . . .

Somewhere there in the middle of the night, I must have made up my mind what I was going to do. When the dawn came, I just rose and dressed and without even consciously thinking about it, I packed my small overnight case, putting in my parents' wedding picture which I had retrieved from a trunk in the attic, all the socks I had, two books from the library which were due in three days, one book of my own, and a little stuffed felt doll which I had given to Jason and then taken back from him. I rolled up my printed-rose quilt and tied it in several places with my belts. Then in blue jeans and a ski jacket I tiptoed out to the kitchen with my belongings and looked down at Rufus who thumped his tail hard against the floor and got up. He stood with his chin over his dish waiting for me to break his egg into it. I saw then that I couldn't leave him behind so while he slurped his egg I rolled his rug around the outside of my quilt. Now it was a big sloppy bundle but I didn't care.

Just as I was easing open the kitchen door I remembered I had no money, so I had to carefully put everything down and return to my bedroom. I had had a dollar put away for a long time because there was nothing I wanted to spend it on. Outside in the snowball bush the birds were beginning to cheep and call with a tremendous clatter. They were so noisy I wondered how anyone could sleep through that, and I knew I had to get away quickly.

Rufus was waiting with his head leaning against the kitchen door. He knew we were going for a walk. I wanted to take his dish, but didn't see how I could carry everything. We'd manage somehow. I stepped out into the cool grayness with those birds still clattering and the eastern sky beginning to flag out in streaks of red. It was going to be a warm day, and I knew I wouldn't need the ski jacket. Still, I thought . . . at night . . .

Rufus and I headed towards what I hoped was south. This was vaguely the direction where our old town and old friends were. I had looked at it often enough on the map, but I wasn't sure of just what road to go along. And besides I wanted to stay off the roads. I could picture my father driving along looking for us soon enough, right about breakfast time, I thought, when they would first miss me. But they wouldn't know anything for sure, I told myself, until I remembered I was carrying Rufus' rug.

"That was very stupid of you," I told Rufus severely, "to let me take your old rug when you knew it would give us away."

I walked a few swift steps ahead of him.

"Just for that, I ought to make you go back alone. Without me. Serve you right."

I was very angry. Rufus was hanging his head. The tone of my voice told him he'd done something really bad, but I finally had to forgive him. After all, it had been my own idea.

We used the road only far enough to get us out of town, then I decided we'd better strike across country even though it would be harder traveling, and we would have to climb a lot of fences. It would be safer that way. I soon found out I was right about one thing; it was a lot harder going. We walked through pasture where the ground was spongy and wet and my shoes became waterlogged. We fought our way through brush that kept trying to tear my bundles away from me, and by this time, they really felt heavy. I gave Rufus a sour look, wishing he could carry his own rug at least. We puffed up hills that gave me a stitch in the side, and I noticed that Rufus wasn't holding up too well. He was panting and beginning to lag behind.

By the time the sun was high, I was starving to death. Rufus, at least, had eaten an egg for breakfast, but I hadn't had a bite. And of course by now, I had lost my sense of direction completely. I had no idea which way

was south although I had been keeping my eyes open looking for the moss that is supposed to grow on the north side of trees. I hadn't found any.

Every once in a while we would come close to a farmhouse and there was always trouble. Farmers must keep the meanest dogs in the world. At each place a big shrieking dog would come bounding out at us, and try to pick a fight with Rufus just because we were walking nearby. Rufus would say, "Urrgghh," and show all his teeth with his black lips drawn so far back he looked like a snarling wolf and the farm dogs would back off towards home, but never shut up. I was afraid the farmers might call the police, so we would hurry on.

It was a long time before I saw a country road which I figured was safe enough to walk on. In a couple of miles we came up to a crossroads and a store with one red gas pump squatting to one side and looking like it never had any customers.

I dropped my bundles outside and went into darkness and unfamiliar smells and there was this old farmer-type man dressed in striped overalls sitting on a sack of something. I didn't know what I wanted to buy, but anything would do. He had a small candy counter, so I bought three chocolate bars. I decided that canned dog food

would keep the best for Rufus, so I got seven cans which took all the rest of my money.

"Stranger round here, aren't you, Miss?" the storekeeper said.

I mumbled something and waved backwards, because my mouth was full of stale-tasting candy. He put the cans in a sack and I left, but he followed me to the door and watched very slyly as I had to pick up my suitcase and rolled quilt which left me no way to carry the dog food. I struggled to force it under my arm, but the sack broke and the cans rolled all over the ground. In desperation I knelt and shoved them into my suitcase and Rufus and I marched down the road with the striped overalls watching us all the way.

I could just almost hear him on the telephone, if he had such a thing, saying, "Sheriff, there's a strange gal going down the road with a big old dog and a suitcase full of dog food. Looks mighty suspicious to me." So there was no choice; we had to leave the road and go back to the pastures and farmhouses.

In the middle of the day I knew I couldn't carry that terribly heavy suitcase any further, so I said to Rufus,

"You are going to carry some of your own food inside of you."

We sat down in the shade of some bushes, and I opened the suitcase to get out a couple of the cans. Then I broke into tears from sheer rage. I had forgotten to bring along a can opener.

I cried a long time while Rufus looked at me sadly, laying his heavy head on my knee, and banging his tail, which was full of burrs and briars, against the stony ground.

My vaguely formed idea when we first started out was that we'd make our way back to our old town and maybe one of the old neighbors or even my favorite teacher, Miss Virginia Townsend, would take us in and keep us both if I worked for our board and room. Now I saw clearly that we weren't going to make it. It was over two hundred miles back there, and without even a can opener, well. . . .

We rested for an hour or so while I talked it over with Rufus who was a good listener and always agreed with me.

"You knew it was a long ways when you started out with me, didn't you?"

He thumped his tail once. I guess he was too tired to argue.

"I always understood that dogs knew their own way back to their old homes. Why didn't you lead?"

He looked away down the hill as if he was searching for the right direction.

"If we go back, you know what it means, don't you? They'll all be against us, and you'll certainly have to mind your P's and Q's from here on in!"

He hung his head in shame, but how could you ask a fourteen-year-old dog to walk two hundred miles when he was all worn out from doing about ten?

We stood up and looked out over a valley that faded into a blue haze in the far distance. I picked up the luggage, and we went back down the hill towards the country store. By the time we got there Rufus was limping.

I went into that dim interior again, and the man was back on his sack, just resting and waiting with his legs crossed.

"Thought you'd be back," he said with a snort of choked laughter.

"Could I please use your telephone?" I asked with great dignity.

"In the back there. Ask the Missus." He jerked his head.

I had to go into their living quarters. It seems they lived right there surrounded by all those groceries and hardware and chicken feed and medicine for cows and horses. His Missus was a pleasant, stumpy woman with square glasses, and afer I'd called home, she gave me a glass of lemonade. I had to ask her where we were, and she took the telephone to give my father directions. He was really boiling mad and hollered over the phone at me, "Swanson's Corner! Where in hell is that?"

I went outside to call Rufus, and she let him come into the kitchen for a drink of cold water. While we waited for my father, I tried to think of how to explain all those cans of dog food and the quilt and Rufus' rug, but there didn't seem to be any way. When my father drove up we climbed in and rode all the way home in guilty silence. My stepmother, Alice, must have told him not to say a word.

When we got home my little brothers looked at me fearfully and my father said with a glint in his eye, "Go to your room and stay there. I'll deal with you later."

Nothing more ever came of it which surprised me no end because I waited all week for punishment.

So now it was a month later, or maybe more.

I still kept to myself at school and if a person talked to me, I just turned away because I had nothing to say to any of them.

On the 5th of November it was my birthday. I woke up with poison in my heart and an ache in my throat that I had to keep swallowing because I was remembering my twelfth birthday when my mother had made a dress for me and also bought me *Tales of Robin Hood* which I don't read anymore, but it was the book I had taken with me when Rufus and I ran away.

Breakfast seemed strangely quiet, all the more so because nobody said a thing, not even "Happy Birthday." I knew they had forgotten.

At school, like always, I answered if I was called on, but not otherwise. I ate my lunch by myself and passed most of the day thinking of how many birthdays I would have to live through before Rufus and I could leave again for good. About four more, I decided, then knew with a deep sorrow that Rufus wouldn't last to be eighteen.

When school was out, I turned in the wrong direction from home and headed for a park up on a high bluff. It was pleasant and empty. The trees were dropping their leaves in little piles and a couple of squirrels chased each other around tree trunks like they were on a merry-go-round. I wanted to stay there forever. I wanted the leaves to cover me like little Hansel and Gretel when they were lost in the woods. I wondered if they had had a stepmother who drove them off, and then I said aloud, "No, that isn't fair. You know it isn't Alice's fault. I don't know whose fault it is for feeling so left out of things."

I looked again at the fallen leaves and thought that my family was like the strong tree that would survive the winter, but I was probably one of the lost leaves.

"I didn't expect them to give me any presents," I kicked at the leaves. I propped my chin on my knees and sat for a long time, thinking and because it was getting late, I read my next day's history lesson. Finally it was too hard to read and looking up, I saw it was almost dark and it was a long way home.

I walked home like I always walked, neither slow nor hurrying. It was just too bad if I was late for supper. I didn't want any anyhow.

When I opened the door the house felt strange. My father was sitting in the front room behind his paper which he put aside for a moment, looked at me and said, "Humph!"

Jason came dancing up to me and grabbed me by the hand pulling me to the dining room.

"Where you been, Patty?" he said. "Everybody waited and waited."

Rufus rushed out from the kitchen to greet me as always, but he was wearing a silly little paper hat tied under his chin. I stood in the brightly lighted room and looked around confused. There had obviously been a party. Used paper plates lay all over and the remains of a big frosted cake was crumpled in the center of the table which had a good linen cloth on it. A pile of wrapped presents lay on the sideboard. In the kitchen I could hear Scott chattering to Alice like a little parakeet and Jason, still clutching my hand, was trying to tell me something.

"All your classmates, Patty," he was saying. "All of them. When you dint come home, we had to have the party without you. Your presents are here."

He tried to drag me towards them, but I shucked him off and rushed to my room.

I was pretty shamefaced when Alice came in to see if I wanted supper.

She sat beside me on the bed and patted me on the back.

"It was my fault," she said. "I shouldn't have tried to surprise you. Anyway, come on out and feed Rufus. I think he's going to be sick from all that cake he was given."

So that's how matters stand now.

Nothing is going to change very much. I don't feel quite so mad at the whole world, and I notice my actions towards Alice are a lot friendlier. It doesn't bother me any when the boys call her "Mother." Maybe, sometime, a long time from now, I might start calling her that myself. Maybe, by spring or so, I might start growing myself back on that family tree.

JEAN McCORD

Jean McCord was born in 1924. She lost her parents when she was twelve, and her love of books provided steadiness in a life that was constantly changing. McCord attended sixteen different schools before graduating from high school at fifteen. After college she had, by her own count, at least forty-five different occupations.

Much of McCord's story-writing is based on her memories of the restless years of her growing up. "The Long Way Around" comes from her book *Deep Where the Octopi Lie*.

I HAVE A DREAM

MARTIN LUTHER KING, JR.

I am happy to join with you today in what will go down in history as the greatest demonstration for freedom in the history of our nation.

Fivescore[1] years ago, a great American, in whose symbolic shadow we stand today, signed the Emancipation Proclamation. This momentous decree came as a great beacon light of hope to millions of Negro slaves who had been seared in the flames of withering injustice. It came as a joyous daybreak to end the long night of their captivity.

But one hundred years later, the Negro is still not free; one hundred years later, the life of the Negro is still sadly crippled by the manacles[2] of segregation and the chains of discrimination; one hundred years later, the Negro lives on a lonely island of poverty in the midst of a vast ocean of material prosperity; one hundred years later,

1. **fivescore** [fīv skōr']: one hundred; one score is a group of twenty.
2. **manacles** [man' ə kəlz]: restraints.

the Negro is still languished[3] in the corners of American society and finds himself in exile in his own land.

So we've come here today to dramatize a shameful condition. In a sense we've come to our nation's capital to cash a check. When the architects of our republic wrote the magnificent words of the Constitution and the Declaration of Independence, they were signing a promissory note[4] to which every American was to fall heir. This note was the promise that all men, yes, black men as well as white men, would be guaranteed the unalienable[5] rights of life, liberty, and the pursuit of happiness.

It is obvious today that America has defaulted on this promissory note in so far as her citizens of color are concerned. Instead of

3. **languished** [lang′ gwishd]: suffering in sadness and neglect.
4. **promissory note** [prom′ ə sôr′ ē]: a written promise.
5. **unalienable** [un ā′ lyə nə bəl]: that cannot be given or taken away.

honoring this sacred obligation, America has given the Negro people a bad check; a check which has come back marked "insufficient funds." We refuse to believe that there are insufficient funds in the great vaults of opportunity of this nation. And so we've come to cash this check, a check that will give us upon demand the riches of freedom and the security of justice.

We have also come to this hallowed[6] spot to remind America of the fierce urgency of now. This is no time to engage in the luxury of cooling off or to take the tranquilizing drug of gradualism. Now is the time to make real the promises of democracy; now is the time to rise from the dark and desolate valley of segregation to the sunlit path of racial justice; now is the time to lift our nation from the quicksands of racial injustice to the solid rock of brotherhood; now is the time to make justice a reality for all God's children. It would be fatal for the nation to overlook the urgency of the moment. This sweltering summer of the Negro's legitimate discontent will not pass until there is an invigorating autumn of freedom and equality.

Nineteen sixty-three is not an end, but a beginning. And those who hope that the Negro needed to blow off steam and will now be content, will have a rude awakening if the nation returns to business as usual.

There will be neither rest nor tranquility in America until the Negro is granted his citizenship rights. The whirlwinds of revolt will continue to shake the foundations of our nation until the bright day of justice emerges.

But there is something that I must say to my people who stand on the warm threshold which leads into the palace of justice. In the process of gaining our rightful place we must not be guilty of wrongful deeds.

Let us not seek to satisfy our thirst for freedom by drinking from the cup of bitterness and hatred. We must forever conduct our struggle on the high plane of dignity and discipline. We must not allow our creative protest to degenerate into physical violence. Again and again we must rise to the majestic heights of meeting physical force with soul force.

6. **hallowed** [hal′ ōd]: holy, sacred.

The marvelous new militancy which has engulfed the Negro community must not lead us to a distrust of all white people, for many of our white brothers, as evidenced by their presence here today, have come to realize that their destiny is tied up with our destiny and they have come to realize that their freedom is inextricably bound to our freedom. This offense we share mounted to storm the battlements of injustice must be carried forth by a biracial army. We cannot walk alone.

And as we walk, we must make the pledge that we shall always march ahead. We cannot turn back. There are those who are asking the devotees of civil rights, "When will you be satisfied?" We can never be satisfied as long as the Negro is the victim of the unspeakable horrors of police brutality.

We can never be satisfied as long as our bodies, heavy with fatigue of travel, cannot gain lodging in the motels of the highways and the hotels of the cities. We cannot be satisfied as long as the Negro's basic mobility is from a smaller ghetto to a larger one.

We can never be satisfied as long as our children are stripped of their selfhood and robbed of their dignity by signs stating "for whites only." We cannot be satisfied as long as a Negro in Mississippi cannot vote and a Negro in New York believes he has nothing for which to vote. No, we are not satisfied, and we will not be satisfied until justice rolls down like waters and righteousness like a mighty stream.

I am not unmindful that some of you come here out of excessive trials and tribulation. Some of you have come fresh from narrow jail cells. Some of you have come from areas where your quest for freedom left you battered by the storms of persecution and staggered by the winds of police brutality. You have been the veterans of creative suffering. Continue to work with the faith that unearned suffering is redemptive.

Go back to Mississippi; go back to Alabama; go back to South Carolina; go back to Georgia; go back to Louisiana; go back to the slums and ghettos of the northern cities, knowing that somehow this situation can, and will be changed. Let us not wallow in the valley of despair.

So I say to you, my friends, that even though we must face the difficulties of today and tomorrow, I still have a dream. It is a dream deeply rooted in the American dream that one day this nation will rise up and live out the true meaning of its creed—we hold these truths to be self-evident, that all men are created equal.

I have a dream that one day on the red hills of Georgia, sons of former slaves and sons of former slave-owners will be able to sit down together at the table of brotherhood.

I have a dream that one day, even the state of Mississippi, a state sweltering with the heat of injustice, sweltering with the heat of oppression, will be transformed into an oasis of freedom and justice.

I have a dream my four little children will one day live in a nation where they will not be judged by the color of their skin but by the content of their character. I have a dream today!

I have a dream that one day, down in Alabama, with its vicious racists, with its governor[7] having his lips dripping with the words of interposition[8] and nullification,[9] that one day, right there in Alabama, little black boys and black girls will be able to join hands with little white boys and white girls as sisters and brothers. I have a dream today!

I have a dream that one day every valley shall be exalted, every hill and mountain shall be made low, the rough places shall be made plain, and the crooked places shall be made straight and the glory of the Lord will be revealed and all flesh shall see it together.

This is our hope. This is the faith that I go back to the South with.

With this faith we will be able to hew out of the mountain of despair a stone of hope. With this faith we will be able to transform the jangling discords of our nation into a beautiful symphony of brotherhood.

With this faith we will be able to work together, to pray together, to struggle together, to go to jail together, to stand up for freedom together, knowing that we will be free one day. This will be the day when all of God's children will be able to sing with new meaning—"my country 'tis of thee; sweet land of liberty; of thee I sing; land where my fathers died, land of the pilgrim's pride; from

7. **governor:** reference to George Wallace, governor of Alabama, who in 1963 opposed school integration.
8. **interposition** [in tər pə zish′ ən]: interruption, interference.
9. **nullification** [nul′ ə fə kā′ shən]: act of causing something to cease to exist.

every mountainside, let freedom ring"—and if America is to be a great nation, this must become true.

So let freedom ring from the prodigious hilltops of New Hampshire.

Let freedom ring from the mighty mountains of New York.

Let freedom ring from the heightening Alleghenies of Pennsylvania.

Let freedom ring from the snow-capped Rockies of Colorado.

Let freedom ring from the curvaceous slopes of California.

But not only that.

Let freedom ring from Stone Mountain of Georgia.

Let freedom ring from Lookout Mountain of Tennessee.

Let freedom ring from every hill and molehill of Mississippi, from every mountainside, let freedom ring.

And when we allow freedom to ring, when we let it ring from every village and hamlet, from every state and city, we will be able to speed up that day when all of God's children—black men and white men, Jews and Gentiles, Catholics and Protestants—will be able to join hands and sing in the words of the old Negro spiritual, "Free at last, free at last; thank God Almighty, we are free at last."

MARTIN LUTHER KING, JR.

Martin Luther King, Jr. [1928-1968], was born in Atlanta, Georgia. He skipped ninth and twelfth grades and entered college when he was only 15 years old. He became a Baptist minister and later earned a Ph.D. in theology. King became a national figure during the civil rights movement of the 1960s. Advocating nonviolent protest he led many of the demonstrations for equal rights that helped to end segregation. In Birmingham, Alabama, where violence flared against the demonstrators, King was jailed for his role as leader.

After the Civil Rights Act passed, King was awarded the Nobel Peace Prize. Four years later, his assassination stunned the world.

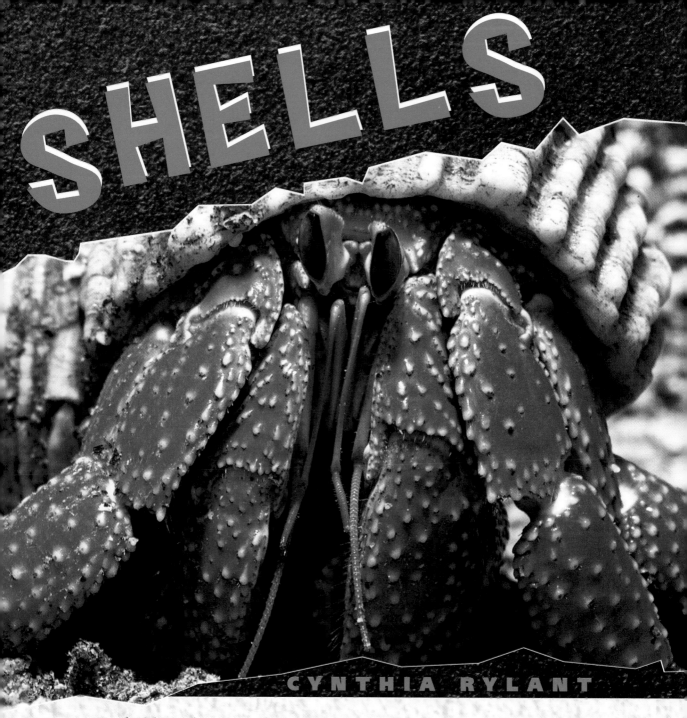

SHELLS

CYNTHIA RYLANT

"You *hate* living here."

Michael looked at the woman speaking to him.

"No, Aunt Esther. I don't." He said it dully, sliding his milk glass back and forth on the table. "I don't hate it here."

Esther removed the last pan from the dishwasher and hung it above the oven.

"You hate it here," she said, "and you hate me."

"I don't!" Michael yelled. "It's not *you!*"

The woman turned to face him in the kitchen.

"Don't yell at me!" she yelled. "I'll not have it in my home. I can't make you happy, Michael. You just refuse to be happy here. And you punish me every day for it."

"*Punish* you?" Michael gawked[1] at her. "I don't punish you! I don't care about you! I don't care what you eat or how you dress or where you go or what you think. Can't you just leave me alone?"

He slammed down the glass, scraped his chair back from the table and ran out the door.

"Michael!" yelled Esther.

They had been living together, the two of them, for six months. Michael's parents had died and only Esther could take him in—or, only she had offered to. Michael's other relatives could not imagine dealing with a fourteen-year-old boy. They wanted peaceful lives.

Esther lived in a condominium in a wealthy section of Detroit. Most of the area's residents were older (like her) and afraid of the world they lived in (like her). They stayed indoors much of the time. They trusted few people.

Esther liked living alone. She had never married or had children. She had never lived anywhere but Detroit. She liked her condominium.

But she was fiercely loyal to her family, and when her only sister had died, Esther insisted she be allowed to care for Michael. And Michael, afraid of going anywhere else, had accepted.

Oh, he was lonely. Even six months after their deaths, he still expected to see his parents—sitting on the couch as he walked into Esther's living room, waiting for the bathroom as he came out of the shower, coming in the door late at night. He still smelled his father's Old Spice somewhere, his mother's talc.

Sometimes he was so sure one of them was *somewhere* around him that he thought maybe he was going crazy. His heart hurt him. He wondered if he would ever get better.

And though he denied it, he did hate Esther. She was so different from his mother and father. Prejudiced—she admired only those who

---

1. **gawked** [gôkd]: stared idly or rudely.

were white and Presbyterian.[2] Selfish—she wouldn't allow him to use her phone. Complaining—she always had a headache or a backache or a stomachache.

He didn't want to, but he hated her. And he didn't know what to do except lie about it.

Michael hadn't made any friends at his new school, and his teachers barely noticed him. He came home alone every day and usually found Esther on the phone. She kept in close touch with several other women in nearby condominiums.

Esther told her friends she didn't understand Michael. She said she knew he must grieve for his parents, but why punish her? She said she thought she might send him away if he couldn't be nicer. She said she didn't deserve this.

But when Michael came in the door, she always quickly changed the subject.

One day after school Michael came home with a hermit crab.[3] He had gone into a pet store, looking for some small, living thing, and hermit crabs were selling for just a few dollars. He'd bought one, and a bowl.

Esther, for a change, was not on the phone when he arrived home. She was having tea and a crescent roll and seemed cheerful. Michael wanted badly to show someone what he had bought. So he showed her.

Esther surprised him. She picked up the shell and poked the long, shiny nail of her little finger at the crab's claws.

"Where is he?" she asked.

Michael showed her the crab's eyes peering through the small opening of the shell.

"Well, for heaven's sake, come out of there!" she said to the crab, and she turned the shell upside down and shook it.

"Aunt Esther!" Michael grabbed for the shell.

"All right, all right." She turned it right side up. "Well," she said, "what does he do?"

2. **Presbyterian** [prez′ bə tir′ ē ən]: belonging to the Presbyterian Church, a Protestant Christian church denomination.
3. **hermit crab:** a crab with a soft body; often lives in the empty shells of snails for protection.

Michael grinned and shrugged his shoulders.

"I don't know," he answered. "Just grows, I guess."

His aunt looked at him.

"An attraction to a crab is something I cannot identify with. However, it's fine with me if you keep him, as long as I can be assured he won't grow out of that bowl." She gave him a hard stare.

"He won't," Michael answered. "I promise."

The hermit crab moved into the condominium. Michael named him Sluggo and kept the bowl beside his bed. Michael had to watch the bowl for very long periods of time to catch Sluggo with his head poking out of his shell, moving around. Bedtime seemed to be Sluggo's liveliest part of the day, and Michael found it easy to lie and watch the busy crab as sleep slowly came on.

One day Michael arrived home to find Esther sitting on the edge of his bed, looking at the bowl. Esther usually did not intrude in Michael's room, and seeing her there disturbed him. But he stood at the doorway and said nothing.

Esther seemed perfectly comfortable, although she looked over at him with a frown on her face.

"I think he needs a companion," she said.

"What?" Michael's eyebrows went up as his jaw dropped down.

Esther sniffed.

"I think Sluggo needs a girl friend." She stood up. "Where is that pet store?"

Michael took her. In the store was a huge tank full of hermit crabs.

"Oh my!" Esther grabbed the rim of the tank and craned her neck over the side. "Look at them!"

Michael was looking more at his Aunt Esther than at the crabs. He couldn't believe it.

"Oh, look at those shells. You say they grow out of them? We must stock up with several sizes. See the pink in that one? Michael, look! He's got his little head out!"

Esther was so dramatic—leaning into the tank, her bangle bracelets clanking, earrings swinging, red pumps clicking on the linoleum—that she attracted the attention of everyone in the store. Michael pretended not to know her well.

He and Esther returned to the condominium with a thirty-gallon tank and twenty hermit crabs.

Michael figured he'd have a heart attack before he got the heavy tank into their living room. He figured he'd die and Aunt Esther would inherit twenty-one crabs and funeral expenses.

But he made it. Esther carried the box of crabs.

"Won't Sluggo be surprised?" she asked happily. "Oh, I do hope we'll be able to tell him apart from the rest. He's their founding father!"

Michael, in a stupor[4] over his Aunt Esther and the phenomenon[5] of twenty-one hermit crabs, wiped out the tank, arranged it with gravel and sticks (as well as the plastic scuba diver Aunt Esther insisted on buying) and assisted her in loading it up, one by one, with the new residents. The crabs were as overwhelmed as Michael. Not one showed its face.

4. **stupor** [stü′ pər]: a dazed condition.
5. **phenomenon** [fə nom′ ə non]: an extraordinary occurrence.

Before moving Sluggo from his bowl, Aunt Esther marked his shell with some red fingernail polish so she could distinguish him from the rest. Then she flopped down on the couch beside Michael.

"Oh, what would your mother *think*, Michael, if she could see this mess we've gotten ourselves into!"

She looked at Michael with a broad smile, but it quickly disappeared. The boy's eyes were full of pain.

"Oh, my," she whispered. "I'm sorry."

Michael turned his head away.

Aunt Esther, who had not embraced anyone in years, gently put her arm about his shoulders.

"I am so sorry, Michael. Oh, you must hate me."

Michael sensed a familiar smell then. His mother's talc.

He looked at his aunt.

"No, Aunt Esther." He shook his head solemnly. "I don't hate you."

Esther's mouth trembled and her bangles clanked as she patted his arm. She took a deep, strong breath.

"Well, let's look in on our friend Sluggo," she said.

They leaned their heads over the tank and found him. The crab, finished with the old home that no longer fit, was coming out of his shell.

CYNTHIA RYLANT

Cynthia Rylant was born in 1954 in Hopewell, Virginia, and spent much of her childhood with her grandparents in West Virginia. "With my grandparents," Rylant says, "there was some poverty, but mostly a very rich existence." The rest of her childhood was spent with her mother in the small town of Beaver, West Virginia. The town had no library, and Rylant had little to read. In college, she discovered that she wanted to be a writer.

"It took me about seven books to feel like a writer," Rylant has said. "But I know now that's what I am." Two of her books for young people are *A Blue-Eyed Daisy* and *A Fine White Dust*.

THE SILENT LOBBY

MILDRED PITTS WALTER

The old bus chugged along the Mississippi highway toward Washington, D.C. I shivered from icy winds and from excitement and fear. Excitement about going to Washington and fear that the old bus would stall again on the dark, lonely, icy road and we'd never make it.

Oh, just to sleep. The chug-chug-chugging of the old motor was not smooth enough to make soothing sounds, and I could not forget the words Mama and Papa had said just before me and Papa left to pick up twenty other people who filled the bus.

"It's too dangerous," Mama had said. "They just might bomb that bus."

"They could bomb this house for that matter," Papa said.

"I know," Mama went on. "That's why I don't want you to go. Why can't you just forget about this voting business and let us live in peace?"

"There can be no peace without freedom," Papa said.

"And you think someone is going to give you freedom?" Mama asked with heat in her voice. "Instead of going to Washington, you should be getting a gun to protect us."

"There are ways to win a struggle without bombs and guns. I'm going to Washington and Craig is going with me."

"Craig is too young."

"He's eleven. That's old enough to know what this is all about," Papa insisted.

I knew. It had all started two years ago, in 1963. Papa was getting ready to go into town to register to vote. Just as he was leaving, Mr. Clem, Papa's boss, came and warned Papa that he should not try to register.

"I intend to register," Papa said.

"If you do, I'll have to fire you." Mr. Clem drove away in a cloud of dust.

"You ought not go," Mama said, alarmed. "You know that people have been arrested and beaten for going down there."

"I'm going," Papa insisted.

"Let me go with you, Papa." I was scared, too, and wanted to be with him if he needed help.

"No, you stay and look after your mama and the house till I get back."

Day turned to night, and Papa had not returned. Mama paced the floor. Was Papa in jail? Had he been beaten. We waited, afraid. Finally, I said, "Mama, I'll go find him."

"Oh, no!" she cried. Her fear scared me more, and I felt angry because I couldn't do anything.

At last we heard Papa's footsteps. The look on his face let us know right away that something was mighty wrong.

"What happened, Sylvester?" Mama asked.

"I paid the poll tax,[1] passed the literacy test, but I didn't interpret the state constitution the way they wanted. So they wouldn't register me."

Feeling a sense of sad relief, I said, "Now you won't lose your job."

"Oh, but I will. I tried to register."

Even losing his job didn't stop Papa from wanting to vote. One day he heard about Mrs. Fannie Lou Hamer and the Mississippi Freedom Democratic Party. The Freedom Party registered people without charging a poll tax, without a literacy test, and without people having to tell what the Mississippi Constitution was about.

On election day in 1964, Papa proudly voted for Mrs. Hamer, Mrs. Victoria Grey, and Mrs. Annie Devine to represent the people of the Second Congressional District of Mississippi. Eighty-three thousand other black men and women voted that day, too. Great victory celebrations were held in homes and churches. But the Governor of Mississippi, Paul B. Johnson, declared all of those eighty-three thousand votes of black people illegal. He gave certificates of election to three white men—William Colmer, John Williams, and a Mr. Whittier—to represent the mostly black Second Congressional District.

Members of the Freedom Party were like Papa—they didn't give up. They got busy when the governor threw out their votes. Lawyers from all over the country came to help. People signed affidavits[2] saying that when they tried to register they lost their jobs, they were beaten, and their homes were burned and churches bombed. More than ten thousand people signed petitions to the governor asking him to count their votes. There was never a word from the governor.

My mind returned to the sound of the old bus slowly grinding along. Suddenly the bus stopped. Not again! We'd never make it now. Papa got out in the cold wind and icy drizzling rain and raised the hood. While he worked, we sang and clapped our hands to keep

---

1. **poll tax** [pōl taks]: a tax paid (prior to 1964) by every adult citizen in order to be able to vote.
2. **affidavits** [af′ ə dā′ vitz]: statements written down and sworn to be true.

warm. I could hear Sister Phyllis praying with all her might for our safety. After a while we were moving along again.

I must have finally fallen asleep, for a policeman's voice woke me. "You can't stop here near the Capitol," he shouted.

"Our bus won't go," Papa said.

"If you made it from Mississippi all the way to D.C., you'll make it from here," the policeman barked.

At first the loud voice frightened me. Then, wide awake, sensing the policeman's impatience, I wondered why Papa didn't let him know that we would go as soon as the motor started. But Papa, knowing that old bus, said nothing. He stepped on the starter. The old motor growled and died. Again the policeman shouted, "I said get out of here."

"We'll have to push it," Papa said.

Everyone got off the bus and pushed. Passersby stopped and stared. Finally we were safe on a side street, away from the Capitol with a crowd gathered around us.

"You mean they came all the way from Mississippi in that?" someone in the crowd asked.

Suddenly the old bus looked shabby. I lowered my head and became aware of my clothes: my faded coat too small; my cotton pants too thin. With a feeling of shame, I wished those people would go away.

"What brings you all to the District?" a man called to us.

"We've come to see about seating the people we voted for and elected," Papa answered. "Down home they say our votes don't count, and up here they've gone ahead and seated men who don't represent us. We've come to talk about that."

"So you've come to lobby," a woman shouted. The crowd laughed.

Why were they laughing? I knew that to lobby meant to try to get someone to decide for or against something. Yes, that was why we had come. I wished I could have said to those people who stood gawking at us that the suffering that brought us here was surely nothing to laugh about.

The laughter from the crowd quieted when another woman shouted, "You're too late to lobby. The House of Representatives will vote on that issue this morning."

Too late. That's what had worried me when the old bus kept breaking down. Had we come so far in this cold for nothing? Was it really too late to talk to members of the House of Representatives to persuade them to seat our representatives elected by the Freedom Party, *not* the ones chosen by the governor?

Just then rain began to fall. The crowd quickly left, and we climbed onto our bus. Papa and the others started to talk. What would we do now? Finally, Papa said, "We can't turn back now. We've done too much and come too far."

After more talk we all agreed that we must try to do what we had come to do. Icy rain pelted us as we rushed against cold wind back to the Capitol.

A doorman stopped us on the steps. "May I have your passes?"

"We don't have any," Papa replied.

"Sorry, you have to have passes for seats in the gallery." The doorman blocked the way.

"We're cold in this rain. Let us in," Sister Phyllis cried.

"Maybe we should just go on back home," someone suggested.

"Yes. We can't talk to the legislators now, anyway," another woman said impatiently.

"No," Papa said. "We must stay if we do no more than let them see that we have come all this way."

"But we're getting soaking wet. We can't stand out here much longer," another protested.

"Can't you just let us in out of this cold?" Papa pleaded with the doorman.

"Not without passes." The doorman still blocked the way. Then he said, "There's a tunnel underneath this building. You can go there to get out of the rain."

We crowded into the tunnel and lined up along the sides. My chilled body and hands came to life pressed against the warm walls. Then footsteps and voices echoed through the tunnel. Police. This tunnel . . . a trap! Would they do something to us for trying to get in without passes? I wanted to cry out to Papa, but I could not speak.

The footsteps came closer. Then many people began to walk by.

When they came upon us, they suddenly stopped talking. Only the sound of their feet echoed in the tunnel. Where had they come from? What did they do? "Who are they, Papa?" I whispered.

"Congressmen and women." Papa spoke so softly, I hardly heard him, even in the silence.

They wore warm coats, some trimmed with fur. Their shoes gleamed. Some of them frowned at us. Others glared. Some sighed quickly as they walked by. Others looked at us, then turned their eyes to their shoes. I could tell by a sudden lift of the head and a certain look that some were surprised and scared. And there were a few whose friendly smiles seemed to say, Right on!

I glanced at Papa. How poor he and our friends looked beside those well-dressed people. Their clothes were damp, threadbare, and wrinkled; their shoes were worn and mud stained. But they all stood straight and tall.

My heart pounded. I wanted to call out to those men and women, "Count my papa's vote! Let my people help make laws, too." But I didn't dare speak in that silence.

Could they hear my heart beating? Did they know what was on my mind? "Lord," I prayed, "let them hear us in this silence."

Then two congressmen stopped in front of Papa. I was frightened until I saw smiles on their faces.

"I'm Congressman Ryan from New York," one of them said. Then he introduced a black man: "This is Congressman Hawkins from California."

"I'm Sylvester Saunders. We are here from Mississippi," Papa said.

"We expected you much earlier," Congressman Ryan said.

"Our old bus and bad weather delayed us," Papa explained.

"That's unfortunate. You could've helped us a lot. We worked late into the night lobbying to get votes on your side. But maybe I should say on *our* side." Mr. Ryan smiled.

"And we didn't do very well," Congressman Hawkins said.

"We'll be lucky if we get fifty votes on our side today," Congressman Ryan informed us. "Maybe you would like to come in and see us at work."

"We don't have passes," I said, surprised at my voice.

"We'll see about getting all of you in," Congressman Hawkins promised.

A little later, as we found seats in the gallery, Congressman Gerald Ford from the state of Michigan was speaking. He did not want Mrs. Hamer and other fairly elected members of the Freedom Party seated in the House. He asked his fellow congressmen to stick to the rule of letting only those with credentials from their states be seated in Congress. The new civil rights act[3] would, in time, undo wrongs done to black Americans. But for now, Congress should let the men chosen by Governor Johnson keep their seats and get on with other business.

Then Congressman Ryan rose to speak. How could Congress stick to rules that denied blacks their right to vote in the state of Mississippi? The rule of letting only those with credentials from a segregated state have seats in the House could not *justly* apply here.

I looked down on those men and few women and wondered if they were listening. Did they know about the petitions? I remembered what Congressman Ryan had said: "We'll be lucky if we get fifty. . . ." Only 50 out of 435 elected to the House.

Finally the time came for Congress to vote. Those who wanted to seat Mrs. Hamer and members of the Freedom Democratic Party were to say, yes. Those who didn't want to seat Mrs. Hamer were to say, no.

At every yes vote I could hardly keep from clapping my hands and shouting, "Yea! Yea!" But I kept quiet, counting: thirty, then forty, forty-eight . . . only two more. We would lose badly.

Then something strange happened. Congressmen and congresswomen kept saying "Yes. Yes. Yes." On and on, "Yes." My heart pounded. Could we win? I sat on my hands to keep from clapping. I looked at Papa and the others who had come with us. They all sat on the edge of their seats. They looked as if they could hardly keep from shouting out, too, as more yes votes rang from the floor.

When the voting was over, 148 votes had been cast in our favor.

3. **civil rights act:** a federal law of 1964 that authorized federal action against segregation in employment and in public places.

What had happened? Why had so many changed their minds?

Later, Papa introduced me to Congressman Hawkins. The congressman asked me, "How did you all know that some of us walk through that tunnel from our offices?"

"We didn't know," I answered. "We were sent there out of the rain."

"That's strange," the congressman said. "Your standing there silently made a difference in the vote. Even though we lost this time, some of them now know that we'll keep on lobbying until we win."

I felt proud. Papa had been right when he said to Mama, "There are ways to win a struggle without bombs and guns." We had lobbied in silence and we had been *heard*.

MILDRED PITTS WALTER

Mildred Pitts Walter was born in 1922 in Sweetville, Louisiana. Walter's parents brought her up to believe in herself, despite poverty and the everyday discrimination that they and other African Americans faced in those days. "I always knew that I could do any kind of work," she once said. "And if I set my mind to it, I could do anything I wanted."

Walter worked her way through college, moved to Los Angeles, and became active in the civil rights movement of the 1960s. Later, she began teaching and writing for children and young people. Her books *The Girl on the Outside* and *Because We Are* tell of the civil rights struggle. Another book, *Have a Happy . . .* , celebrates aspects of African American heritage that Walter learned during a trip to Africa.

The

onald leaned into the car trunk to find the box holding the giveaways. He had to pay for each letter opener, shoehorn, and vegetable brush, money out of his own commission,[1] but it was worth it. Why else would people listen to his sales spiel if it wasn't because they felt indebted the second they reached for a sample?

What a mess, he thought, getting grease on his hand. Ever since Mom stopped driving. Ever since she . . .

quits for the day, but maybe he'd work another hour. If he went home now, even though it would mean a real meal, not McDonald's, Ava would be there. Their newest housekeeper, she'd sit there at the kitchen table, arms folded, watching him, and she'd go into her usual song and dance.

"Go in to your mother. Just for a minute. Say hello. Say *something*."

"Later."

"*Now*. She'll be asleep later."

Fuller Brush Man

GLORIA D. MIKLOWITZ

Well, there was no use dwelling on that. When he had time he'd try to get rid of some of the junk. He dropped a dozen plastic shoehorns into his sample case, snapped the lock, and glanced at his watch.

Man, he was hungry. He'd been working steadily since right after school, four hours. All he'd eaten was a doughnut left in the breadbox at home, running out the door with Ava calling after him to get a glass of milk first.

He'd sold enough brushes to call it

"Why? She can't talk. She probably doesn't even know who I am. What difference does it make?"

"Donnie, Donnie. You love her. I know you do. Do it for you, if not for her."

"Leave me alone."

He'd get this picture in his head of Mom, the way she had become lately. Bloated face, dull eyes that followed him without seeming to see, a stomach as if she was pregnant. And her arms skinny, all bones. *Why? How could she do that to him, to them?*

---

1. **commission** [kə mish′ ən]: a percentage of the amount of money earned by a business deal, paid to the agent who does the business.

No. He'd just get a bite nearby and go home later. He could maybe make five more sales. More money for the college fund. And with what Dad was putting out in medical bills and nursing care, every cent counted.

He crossed the street and was nearly knocked down by a kid on a two-wheeler, shooting out of a driveway, wobbling his way down the road. When had *he* learned to ride a bike? Eight, nine years ago? Yes. In the Apperson Street schoolyard, late afternoons. He could hear the crickets chirping even now, and for a second he felt the same surge of fear and exultation[2] he'd felt then gripping the handlebars.

"I can't! I can't! I'm falling! Mom, Mom! Help me!"

"You can! You can! Keep going! That's right! You're doing it!"

Running alongside, face sweating and flushed, red hair flying about her eyes and cheeks, she was laughing with joy. And when he finally managed to stop she threw her arms around him and cried, "See? You did it! I knew you could!"

He swallowed a lump in his throat and marched briskly up the walk to the door of a small, wooden house. He rang the bell and waited, peering through the screen door into a living room with a worn couch, a TV flickering against one wall, and a small child sitting in front of it.

"If you don't behave, you'll have to watch TV," his mother would say when he was that age, as if watching TV was punishment. Maybe that's why he hardly watched even now.

When *he* was little, this was the time of day he loved most. Right after supper and before bedtime. He'd climb up on the couch to sit beside Mom. Bonnie would take her place on Mom's other side and for a half hour it was "weed books" time.

He felt an overwhelming hunger for those times, for Mom's arm around him and her warm voice reading. He wiped a hand across his eyes as a woman, holding a baby, came to the door.

"Fuller brush man! Good evening, missus. Would you like a sample?" Donald held out a brush, a letter opener, and a shoehorn. With but a second's hesitation the woman unlatched the door and stepped forward, eyeing the samples greedily. She took the brush.

"Good choice," Donald said. "They're great for scrubbing vegetables. Now, would you like to see our specials?" He held the catalog open to the specials page, but the light was fading.

---

2. **exultation** [eg′ zul tā′ shən]: a great rejoicing, triumph.

"I don't need any . . ."

"Then maybe you'd like to try our new tile-cleaning foam. See?" He plucked a can from his case and showed her the cap with its stiff bristles for the "hard-to-clean places between the tiles."

"I have Formica."[3]

"Sally? Sally? Who the devil is that?"

"Just a brush salesman, honey!"

"Well, tell him you don't need any!"

The woman gave him a sheepish grin, backed away, and said, "Sorry." She closed the screen door and latched it again.

He used to take rejection hard, getting a pain in his stomach that grew with each door shut in his face, each disgusted "Don't bother me." He still withdrew inside when people turned him away, although he wouldn't show it now, keeping his voice pleasant and a smile on his face. If anyone asked, he'd say he hated the job even though he was learning a lot about human nature and keeping books, and it did pay well.

"Sell door to door?" his mother had asked when he first proposed the idea. "Absolutely not!"

"Why not? I could save what I make for college!"

"No!"

"Why? That's not fair!"

"Because." He watched her struggle to find words for what she hadn't thought out. "Because it's not safe, knocking on strange people's doors. The world is full of crazies. Because I don't want you to have to get doors slammed in your face. Because it will be summer soon and too hot to work outdoors. If you want a job, find one where it's air-conditioned."

"Let him try," Dad said. "One day of it and he'll quit."

"*Please*, Mom?"

"Oh, all right," she conceded, but only because that morning he'd accused her of still treating him like a baby. "But only to try it. *One* day!"

It was three months now. She must have been sick even then, because after that first day when he'd come home triumphant with having made fifty-four dollars in only six hours, he didn't hear anything more about quitting. It was about then that she went into the hospital for the first time and his whole life began to change.

When he finished another block, he circled back to the car, a dog barking at his heels. One of the hazards of selling things in strange neighborhoods was the dogs. He

---

3. **Formica** [fôr mĭ′ kə]: plastic, used on kitchen and furniture surfaces, that resists water, heat, and most chemicals.

carried Mace[4] but hated using it. He found that if he stood his ground and shouted "No," most dogs would go through their ferocious act and run off when they figured they'd done their duty.

In the dim light of the car he looked over his orders and decided to drive down to the boulevard for something to eat. Maybe he'd phone Shannon afterwards, drop by for a few minutes before going home. He started the engine, turned on the headlights, and drove down the hill.

"*H*ow's your Mom?" Shannon asked when he reached her from the phone in the parking lot. There was so much traffic noise he had to press the receiver tight against his ear.

"What are you doing?" he asked in response. "I can be by in ten minutes. We could go for a walk."

"When are you going to talk about it?" Shannon asked. "Bonnie says she's worse. It's awful how you're acting. It's not her fault."

For a second he considered not answering at all, but finally he said, "Stop bugging me. Everyone's after me about it. It's *my* mom. It's my business. If that's all you want to talk about, forget it."

"But, Donnie! You can't put it off much longer."

He hung up without answering and ran back to the car.

Slamming the door, he slumped in the driver's seat and stared out at the ribbon of lights on the freeway. If he let himself think about what Shannon said, he'd just start blubbering like a baby. Better to work. He'd get at the orders for the week. They were due to be toted up and recorded on the big order sheet by tomorrow. Usually he'd work on it at home, spreading the papers out on his desk and marking how many of this or that he'd sold that week. But if he went home now, they'd *all* be there: Dad, Bonnie, and Ava. All accusing. Bonnie with her *Please, Donnie*'s. Ava with her *Why don't you*'s. And Dad with his sad silence, worse than words.

But worst of all was knowing that Mom lay in the next room wasting away, dying, not even fighting anymore. He felt that if he was forced to go in there, all he'd do is scream at her. "Don't you care? Try! You always told us never to give up! You're not trying!" And he'd want to strike out at her. Well, maybe not at her, but at something!

There wasn't a moment in the day that he didn't think about her. It was as if they were joined by an invisible wire

---

4. **Mace** [mās]: a chemical spray containing tear gas.

and he felt everything she did. And he felt now that she was slipping away. He couldn't stop it. He couldn't do a thing about it. There was nothing to say, nothing! Everything he thought of saying sounded false or stupid.

Well, all right! If that's what he had to do, he'd do it. He'd *go* home. He'd go into her room. He'd look at that woman who was and wasn't his mother anymore and he'd say *something*. Whatever came into his head, no matter how mean or dumb. *All right!* If that's what they all wanted, that's what he'd do.

He turned the key in the ignition and gunned the car out of the parking lot and into the street. He drove above the speed limit, mouth clenched in a tight line, totally intent on the road, mind empty except for the determination to get home fast.

He parked the car in the drive and ran into the house. Suddenly he was terribly afraid. What if it was too late? He almost felt in his gut that he'd waited too long.

"Donnie?" Dad called from the family room. "That you?"

He made some kind of guttural response and ran past the room, not even nodding. He had a fleeting sense that Dad was there reading the paper, that Bonnie was doing homework. His heart hammered loudly in his ears. An electrical pulse ran down his arms to his legs as he reached his mother's bedroom door and put a hand on the knob.

And then he stopped. For a long moment he stood waiting for his legs to quit trembling, for his heart to slow down. And then he closed his eyes, took a deep breath, and straightened his shoulders. Fixing a smile on his face, he knocked. "Fuller brush man!" he called, lightly opening the door.

GLORIA D. MIKLOWITZ

Gloria D. Miklowitz was born in 1927 in New York City. Before she began writing for young people, she says, she wrote documentary films on rockets and torpedoes for the Navy.

Miklowitz says she enjoys writing because it lets her "live hundreds of different lives . . . . On paper . . . I enter lives I can never really live and try to bring to my readers compassion and understanding for those lives."

Miklowitz has written more than thirty books about problems young adults face. Her books have been translated into many languages. Two of her books are *Anything to Win* and *The Emerson High Vigilantes.*

BROWN VS. BOARD OF EDUCATION

WALTER DEAN MYERS

Thurgood Marshall as a young man

There was a time when the meaning of freedom was easily understood. For an African crouched in the darkness of a tossing ship, wrists chained, men with guns standing on the decks above him, freedom was a physical thing, the ability to move away from his captors, to follow the dictates of his own heart, to listen to the voices within him that defined his values and showed him the truth of his own path. The plantation owners wanted to make the Africans feel helpless, inferior. They denied them images of themselves as Africans and told them that they were without beauty. They segregated them and told them they were without value.

Slowly, surely, the meaning of freedom changed to an elusive thing that even the strongest people could not hold in their hands. There were no chains on black wrists, but there were the shadows of chains, stretching for hundreds of years back through time, across black minds.

From the end of the Civil War in 1865 to the early 1950's, many public schools in both the North and South were segregated. Segregation was different in the different sections of the country. In the North most of the schools were segregated *de facto;*[1] that is, the law allowed blacks and whites to go to school together, but they did not actually always attend the same schools. Since a school is generally attended by children living in its neighborhood, wherever there were predominantly African-American neighborhoods there were, "in fact," segregated schools. In many parts of the country, however, and especially in the South, the segregation was *de jure,*[2] meaning that there were laws which forbade blacks to attend the same schools as whites.

The states with segregated schools relied upon the ruling of the Supreme Court in the 1896 *Plessy vs. Ferguson* case for legal justification: Facilities that were "separate but equal" were legal.

In the early 1950's the National Association for the Advancement of Colored People (N.A.A.C.P.) sponsored five cases that eventually reached the Supreme Court. One of the cases involved the school board of Topeka, Kansas.

Thirteen families sued the Topeka school board, claiming that to segregate the children was harmful to the children and, therefore, a violation of the equal protection clause of the Fourteenth Amendment.[3] The names on the Topeka case were listed in alphabetical order, with the father of seven-year-old Linda Brown listed first.

1. *de facto* [di fak′ tō]: in fact, in reality.
2. *de jure* [dē jùr′ ē]: by right, according to law.
3. **Fourteenth Amendment:** the constitutional amendment (1868) guaranteeing equal protection under the law for all those born or naturalized in the United States, including former slaves.

I didn't understand why I couldn't go to school with my playmates. I lived in an integrated neighborhood and played with children of all nationalities, but when school started they went to a school only four blocks from my home and I was sent to school across town,

she says.

For young Linda the case was one of convenience and of being made to feel different, but for African-American parents it had been a long, hard struggle to get a good education for their children. It was also a struggle waged by lawyers who had worked for years to overcome segregation. The head of the legal team who presented the school cases was Thurgood Marshall.[4]

The city was Baltimore, Maryland, and the year was 1921. Thirteen-year-old Thurgood Marshall struggled to balance the packages he was carrying with one hand while he tried to get his bus fare out of his pocket with the other. It was almost Easter, and the part-time job he had would provide money for flowers for his mother. Suddenly he felt a violent tug at his right arm that spun him around, sending his packages sprawling over the floor of the bus.

"Nigguh, don't you never push in front of no white lady again!" an angry voice spat in his ear.

Thurgood turned and threw a punch into the face of the name caller. The man charged into Thurgood, throwing punches that mostly missed, and tried to wrestle the slim boy to the ground. A policeman broke up the fight, grabbing Thurgood with one huge black hand and pushing him against the side of the bus. Within minutes they were in the local courthouse.

Thurgood was not the first of his family to get into a good fight. His father's father had joined the Union Army during the Civil War, taking the names Thorough Good to add to the one name he had in bondage. His grandfather on his mother's side was a man brought

4. **Thurgood Marshall** [thėr′ gůd mär shəl]: (1908-1993) African American civil rights leader, chief legal counsel for the NAACP, and a Supreme Court justice.

from Africa and, according to Marshall's biography, "so ornery that his owner wouldn't sell him out of pity for the people who might buy him, but gave him his freedom instead and told him to clear out of the county."

Thurgood's frequent scrapes earned him a reputation as a young boy who couldn't be trusted to get along with white folks.

Thurgood Marshall's parents

His father, Will Marshall, was a steward at the Gibson Island Yacht Club near Baltimore, and his mother, Norma, taught in a segregated school. The elder Marshall felt he could have done more with his life if his education had been better, but there had been few opportunities available for African Americans when he had been a young man. When it was time for the Marshall boys to go to college, he was more than willing to make the sacrifices necessary to send them.

Young people of color from all over the world came to the United States to study at Lincoln University, a predominantly black institution in southeastern Pennsylvania. Here Marshall majored in pre-dentistry, which he found boring, and joined the Debating Club, which he found interesting. By the time he was graduated at the age of twenty-one, he had decided to give up dentistry for the law. Three years later he was graduated, first in his class, from Howard University Law School.

At Howard there was a law professor, Charles Hamilton Houston, who would affect the lives of many African-American lawyers and who would influence the legal aspects of the civil rights movement. Houston was a great teacher, one who demanded that his students be not just good lawyers but great lawyers. If they were going

Thurgood Marshall with Central High School students from Little Rock, Arkansas, September, 1957

to help their people—and for Houston the only reason for African Americans to become lawyers was to do just that—they would have to have absolute understanding of the law, and be diligent in the preparation of their cases. At the time, Houston was an attorney for the N.A.A.C.P. and fought against discrimination in housing and in jobs.

After graduation, Thurgood Marshall began to do some work for the N.A.A.C.P., trying the difficult civil rights cases. He not only knew about the effects of discrimination by reading about it, he was still living it when he was graduated from law school in 1933. In 1936 Marshall began working full-time for the N.A.A.C.P., and in 1940 became its chief counsel.

It was Thurgood Marshall and a battery of N.A.A.C.P. attorneys who began to challenge segregation throughout the country. These men and women were warriors in the cause of freedom for African Americans, taking their battles into courtrooms across the country. They understood the process of American justice and the power of the Constitution.

In *Brown vs. Board of Education of Topeka*, Marshall argued that segregation was a violation of the Fourteenth Amendment—that even if the facilities and all other "tangibles"[5] were equal, which was the heart of the case in *Plessy vs. Ferguson*, a violation still existed. There were intangible factors, he argued, that made the education unequal.

Everyone involved understood the significance of the case: that it was much more than whether black children could go to school with white children. If segregation in the schools was declared unconstitutional, then *all* segregation in public places could be declared unconstitutional.

5. **tangibles** [tan′ jə bəlz]: whatever is real and can be touched, such as property and money.

Southerners who argued against ending school segregation were caught up, as then-Congressman Brooks Hays of Arkansas put it, in "a lifetime of adventures in that gap between law and custom." The law was one thing, but most Southern whites felt just as strongly about their customs as they did the law.

Dr. Kenneth B. Clark, an African-American psychologist, testified for the N.A.A.C.P. He presented clear evidence that the effect of segregation was harmful to African-American children. Describing studies conducted by black and white psychologists over a twenty-year period, he showed that black children felt inferior to white children. In a particularly dramatic study that he had supervised, four dolls, two white and two black, were presented to African-American children. From the responses of the children to the dolls, identical in every way except color, it was clear that the children were rejecting the black dolls. African-American children did not just feel separated from white children, they felt that the separation was based on their inferiority.

Dr. Clark understood fully the principles and ideas of those people who had held Africans in bondage and had tried to make slaves of captives. By isolating people of African descent, by barring them from certain actions or places, they could make them feel inferior. The social scientists who testified at *Brown vs. Board of Education* showed that children who felt inferior also performed poorly.

The Justice Department argued that racial segregation was objectionable to the Eisenhower Administration and hurt our relationships with other nations.

On May 17, 1954, after deliberating for nearly a year and a half, the Supreme Court made its ruling. The Court stated that it could not use the intentions of 1868, when the Fourteenth Amendment was passed, as a guide to its ruling, or even those of 1896, when the decision in *Plessy vs. Ferguson* was handed down. Chief Justice Earl Warren wrote:

We must consider public education in the light of its full development and its present place in American life throughout the nation. We must look

Thurgood Marshall,
Supreme Court Justice

instead to the effect of segregation itself on public education.

The Court went on to say that "modern authority" supported the idea that segregation deprived African Americans of equal opportunity. "Modern authority" referred to Dr. Kenneth B. Clark and the weight of evidence that he and the other social scientists had presented.

The high court's decision in *Brown vs. Board of Education* signaled an important change in the struggle for civil rights. It signaled clearly that the legal prohibitions that oppressed African Americans would have to fall. Equally important was the idea that the nature of the fight for equality would change. Ibrahima,[6] Cinqué,[7] Nat Turner,[8] and George Latimer[9] had struggled for freedom by fighting against their captors or fleeing from them. The 54th[10] had fought for African freedom on the battlefields of the Civil War. Ida B. Wells[11] had fought for equality with her pen.

6. **Ibrahima** [ē brä hē mä]: (1762-1829) African prince who became a slave, later obtained his freedom, and returned to West Africa.
7. **Cinqué** [singk ā′]: African slave, sold in 1839, who took command of a slave ship, was captured, tried in Connecticut, and freed; he later returned to West Africa.
8. **Nat Turner:** a slave of the early 1800s who led the only effective slave revolt in the United States; he was captured and hanged in 1831.
9. **George Latimer:** African slave who escaped in Boston in 1842 and led the first of several fugitive slave uprisings.
10. **54th:** African American regiment from Massachusetts during the War Between the States.
11. **Ida B. Wells:** African American woman, editor of the Memphis newspaper *Free Speech*, who worked for civil rights from the late 1800s until her death in 1931.

Lewis H. Latimer[12] and Meta Vaux Warrick[13] had tried to earn equality with their work. In *Brown vs. Board of Education* Thurgood Marshall, Kenneth B. Clark, and the lawyers and social scientists, both black and white, who helped them had won for African Americans a victory that would bring them closer to full equality than they had ever been in North America. There would still be legal battles to be won, but the major struggle would be in the hearts and minds of people and "in that gap between law and custom."

In 1967 Thurgood Marshall was appointed by President Lyndon B. Johnson as an associate justice of the U.S. Supreme Court. He retired in 1991.

"I didn't think of my father or the other parents as being heroic at the time," Linda Brown says. "I was only seven. But as I grew older and realized how far-reaching the case was and how it changed the complexion of the history of this country, I was just thrilled that my father and the others here in Topeka were involved."

12. **Lewis H. Latimer:** African American, son of an escaped slave, who invented the carbon filament for the incandescent lamp, patented in 1881; he was also a poet, painter, and civil rights worker.
13. **Meta Vaux Warrick** [me′ tə vō wô′ rik]: African American woman artist of the late 1800s and early 1900s who studied art in Paris.

WALTER DEAN MYERS

Walter Dean Myers was born in 1937 in Martinsburg, West Virginia, but grew up on the streets of Harlem in New York City. In high school, Myers found that literature offered a "connection with things and events that I was not part of in 'real' life."

Since his family couldn't afford to send him to college, Myers went into the Army. Later he took various jobs to get by until he could support himself as a full-time writer. Myers is best known for novels such as *The Young Landlords* and *The Outside Shot*. His nonfiction books include *Now Is Your Time: The African American Struggle for Freedom* and *The World of Work: A Guide to Choosing a Career*.

It fell about the Martinmas[1] time,
    And a gay time it was then,
When our goodwife got puddings to make,
    And she's boiled them in the pan.

The wind so cold blew south and north,   5
    And blew into the floor;
Quoth our goodman to our goodwife,
    "Get up and bar the door."

"My hand is in my household work,
    Goodman, as ye may see;   10
And it will not be barred for a hundred years,
    If it's to be barred by me!"

They made a pact between them both,
    They made it firm and sure,
That whosoe'er should speak the first,   15
    Should rise and bar the door.

Then by there came two gentlemen,
    At twelve o'clock at night,
And they could see neither house nor hall,
    Nor coal nor candlelight.   20

1. **Martinmas** [mär′ tn məs]: a Roman
   Catholic feast day, celebrated
   November 11, to honor Saint Martin
   (1250-1300).

"Now whether is this a rich man's house,
 Or whether is it a poor?"
But never a word would one of them speak,
 For barring of the door.

The guests they ate the white puddings, 25
 And then they ate the black;
Tho' much the goodwife thought to herself,
 Yet never a word she spake.

Then said one stranger to the other,
 "Here, man, take ye my knife; 30
Do ye take off the old man's beard,
 And I'll kiss the goodwife."

"There's no hot water to scrape it off,
 And what shall we do then?"
"Then why not use the pudding broth, 35
 That boils into the pan?"

O up then started our goodman,
 An angry man was he;
"Will ye kiss my wife before my eyes?
 And with pudding broth scald me?" 40

Then up and started our goodwife,
 Gave three skips on the floor;
"Goodman, you've spoken the foremost[2] word.
 Get up and bar the door."

2. foremost [fôr′ mōst]: first.

The Necklace

Boulevard Montmartre on a Winter Day Camille Jacob Pissarro, 1897, oil on canvas, 25 1/2" x 32", Metropolitan Museum of Art, New York (Detail on page 96)

GUY DE MAUPASSANT

he was one of those pretty, charming young ladies born, as if through an error of destiny, into a family of clerks. She had no dowry, no hopes, no means of becoming known, appreciated, loved, and married by a man either rich or distinguished; and she allowed herself to marry a petty clerk in the office of the Board of Education.

She was simple, not being able to adorn herself; but she was unhappy, as one out of her class; for women belong to no caste, no race; their grace, their beauty, and their charm serving them in the place of birth and family. Their inborn finesse, their instinctive elegance, their suppleness of wit are their only aristocracy, making some daughters of the people the equal of great ladies.

She suffered incessantly, feeling herself born for all delicacies and luxuries. She suffered from the poverty of her apartment, the shabby walls, the worn chairs, and the faded stuffs. All these things, which another woman of her station would not have noticed, tortured and angered her. The sight of the little Breton, who made this humble home, awoke in her sad regrets and desperate dreams. She thought of quiet antechambers[1], with their Oriental hangings, lighted by high, bronze torches, and of the two great footmen in short trousers who sleep in the large armchairs, made sleepy by the heavy air from the heating apparatus. She thought of large drawingrooms, hung in old silks, of graceful pieces of furniture carrying bric-à-brac[2] of inestimable value, and of the little perfumed coquettish[3] apartments, made for five o'clock chats with most intimate friends, men known and sought after, whose attention all women envied and desired.

When she seated herself for dinner, before the round table where the tablecloth had been used three days, opposite her husband who uncovered the tureen with a delighted air, saying: "Oh! the good potpie! I know nothing better than that—" she would think of the elegant dinners, of the shining silver, of the tapestries peopling the walls with ancient personages and rare birds in the midst of fairy forests; she thought of the exquisite food served on marvelous dishes, of the whispered gallantries, listened to with the smile of the sphinx, while eating the rose-colored flesh of the trout or a chicken's wing.

She had neither frocks nor jewels, nothing. And she loved only those things. She felt that she was made for them. She had such a desire to please, to be sought after, to be clever, and courted.

She had a rich friend, a schoolmate at the convent whom she did not like to visit, she suffered so much when she returned. And

1. **antechambers** [an′ ti chām′ bərz]: small waiting rooms.
2. **bric-à-brac** [brik′ ə brak′]: curious decorative ornaments, such as vases or china.
3. **coquettish** [kō ket′ ish]: attracting attention.

she wept for whole days from chagrin, from regret, from despair, and disappointment.

One evening her husband returned elated, bearing in his hand a large envelope.

"Here," said he, "here is something for you."

She quickly tore open the wrapper and drew out a printed card on which were inscribed these words:

"The Minister of Public Instruction and Madame George Ramponneau[4] ask the honor of Mr. and Mrs. Loisel's[5] company Monday evening, January 18, at the Minister's residence."

Instead of being delighted, as her husband had hoped, she threw the invitation spitefully upon the table murmuring:

"What do you suppose I want with that?"

"But, my dearie, I thought it would make you happy. You never go out, and this is an occasion, and a fine one! I had a great deal of trouble to get it. Everybody wishes one, and it is very select; not many are given to employees. You will see the whole official world there."

4. **Ramponneau** [räM pô nō′]
5. **Loisel** [lwä zel′]

She looked at him with an irritated eye and declared impatiently:

"What do you suppose I have to wear to such a thing as that?"

He had not thought of that; he stammered:

"Why, the dress you wear when we go to the theater. It seems very pretty to me—"

He was silent, stupefied, in dismay, at the sight of his wife weeping. Two great tears fell slowly from the corners of his eyes toward the corners of his mouth; he stammered:

"What is the matter? What is the matter?"

By a violent effort, she had controlled her vexation and responded in a calm voice, wiping her moist cheeks:

"Nothing. Only I have no dress and consequently I cannot go to this affair. Give your card to some colleague whose wife is better fitted out than I."

He was grieved, but answered:

"Let us see, Matilda. How much would a suitable costume cost, something that would serve for other occasions, something very simple?"

She reflected for some seconds, making estimates and thinking of a sum that she could ask for without bringing with it an immediate refusal

and a frightened exclamation from the economical clerk.

Finally she said, in a hesitating voice:

"I cannot tell exactly, but it seems to me that four hundred francs ought to cover it."

He turned a little pale, for he had saved just this sum to buy a gun that he might be able to join some hunting parties the next summer, on the plains at Nanterre, with some friends who went to shoot larks up there on Sunday. Nevertheless, he answered:

"Very well. I will give you four hundred francs. But try to have a pretty dress."

The day of the ball approached and Mme. Loisel seemed sad, disturbed, anxious. Nevertheless, her dress was nearly ready. Her husband said to her one evening:

"What is the matter with you? You have acted strangely for two or three days."

And she responded: "I am vexed not to have a jewel, not one stone, nothing to adorn myself with. I shall have such a poverty-laden look. I would prefer not to go to this party."

He replied: "You can wear some natural flowers. At this season they look very chic. For ten francs you can have two or three magnificent roses."

She was not convinced. "No," she replied, "there is nothing more humiliating than to have a shabby air in the midst of rich women."

Then her husband cried out: "How stupid we are! Go and find your friend Mrs. Forestier and ask her to lend you her jewels. You are well enough acquainted with her to do this."

She uttered a cry of joy: "It is true!" she said. "I had not thought of that."

The next day she took herself to her friend's house and related her story of distress. Mrs. Forestier went to her closet with the glass doors, took out a large jewel-case, brought it, opened it, and said: "Choose, my dear."

She saw at first some bracelets, then a collar of pearls, then a Venetian cross of gold and jewels and of admirable workmanship. She tried the jewels before the glass, hesitated, but could neither decide to take them nor leave them. Then she asked:

"Have you nothing more?"

"Why, yes. Look for yourself. I do not know what will please you."

Suddenly she discovered, in a black satin box, a supurb necklace of diamonds, and her heart beat fast with an immoderate desire. Her hands trembled as she took them up. She placed them about her throat

against her dress, and remained in ecstasy before them. Then she asked, in a hesitating voice, full of anxiety:

"Could you lend me this? Only this?"

"Why, yes, certainly."

She fell upon the neck of her friend, embraced her with passion, then went away with her treasure.

The day of the ball arrived. Mme Loisel was a great success. She was the prettiest of all, el-egant, gracious, smiling, and full of joy. All the men noticed her, asked her name, and wanted to be presented. All the members of the Cabinet wished to waltz with her. The Minister of Education paid her some attention.

She danced with enthusiasm, with passion, intoxicated with pleasure, thinking of nothing, in the triumph of her beauty, in the glory of her success, in a kind of cloud of happiness that came of all this homage, and all this admira-tion, of all these awakened desires, and this victory so complete and sweet to the heart of woman.

She went home toward four o'clock in the morning. Her husband had been half asleep in one of the little salons since midnight, with three other gentlemen whose wives were enjoying themselves very much.

He threw around her shoulders the wraps they had carried for the coming home, modest garments of everyday wear, whose poverty clashed with the elegance of the ball costume. She felt this and wished to hurry away in order not to be noticed by the other women who were wrapping them-selves in rich furs.

Loisel retained her: "Wait," said he. "You will catch cold out there. I am go-ing to call a cab."

But she would not listen and de-scended the steps rapidly. When they were in the street, they found no carriage; and they began to seek one, hailing the coachmen whom they saw at a distance.

They walked along toward the Seine,[6] hopeless and shivering. Finally they found on the dock one of those old, nocturnal coupés[7] that one sees in Paris after nightfall, as if they were ashamed of their misery by day.

---

6. **Seine** [sān]: a river that flows from Eastern France to the English Channel.
7. **coupés** [kü pāz′]: closed, horse-drawn carriages holding passengers inside and the driver outside.

It took them as far as their door in Martyr street, and they went wearily up to their apartment. It was all over for her. And on his part, he remembered that he would have to be at the office by ten o'clock.

She removed the wraps from her shoulders before the glass, for a final view of herself in her glory. Suddenly she uttered a cry. Her necklace was not around her neck.

Her husband, already half undressed, asked: "What is the matter?"

She turned toward him excitedly:

"I have—I have—I no longer have Mrs. Forestier's necklace."

He arose in dismay: "What! How is that? It is not possible."

And they looked in the folds of the dress, in the folds of the mantle, in the pockets, everywhere. They could not find it.

He asked: "You are sure you still had it when we left the house?"

"Yes, I felt it in the vestibule[8] as we came out."

"But if you had lost it in the street, we should have heard it fall. It must be in the cab."

"Yes. It is probable. Did you take the number?"

"No. And you, did you notice what it was?"

"No."

They looked at each other utterly cast down. Finally, Loisel dressed himself again.

"I am going," said he, "over the track where we went on foot, to see if I can find it."

And he went. She remained in her evening gown, not having the force to go to bed, stretched upon a chair, without ambition or thoughts.

Toward seven o'clock her husband returned. He had found nothing.

He went to the police and to the cab offices, and put an advertisement in the newspapers, offering a reward; he did everything that afforded them a suspicion of hope.

She waited all day in a state of bewilderment before this frightful disaster. Loisel returned at evening with his face harrowed and pale; he had discovered nothing.

"It will be necessary," said he, "to write to your friend that you have broken the clasp of the necklace and that you will have it repaired. That will give us time to turn around."

She wrote as he dictated.

At the end of a week, they had lost all hope. And Loisel, older by five years, declared:

"We must take measures to replace this jewel."

8. **vestibule** [ves′ tə byül]: a hall between the outer door and the inside of a building.

The next day they took the box which had inclosed it, to the jeweler whose name was on the inside. He consulted his books:

"It is not I, Madame," said he, "who sold this necklace; I only furnished the casket."

Then they went from jeweler to jeweler seeking a necklace like the other one, consulting their memories, and ill, both of them, with chagrin and anxiety.

In a shop of the Palais-Royal, they found a chaplet[9] of diamonds which seemed to them exactly like the one they had lost. It was valued at forty thousand francs. They could get it for thirty-six thousand.

They begged the jeweler not to sell it for three days. And they made an arrangement by which they might return it for thirty-four thousand francs if they found the other one before the end of February.

Loisel possessed eighteen thousand francs which his father had left him. He borrowed the rest.

He borrowed it, asking for a thousand francs of one, five hundred of another, five louis[10] of this one, and three louis of that one. He gave notes, made ruinous promises, took

money of usurers and the whole race of lenders. He compromised his whole existence, in fact, risked his signature, without even knowing whether he could make it good or not, and, harassed by anxiety for the future, by the black misery which surrounded him, and by the prospect of all physical privations and moral torture, he went to get the new necklace, depositing on the merchant's counter thirty-six thousand francs.

When Mrs. Loisel took back the jewels to Mrs. Forestier, the latter said to her in a frigid tone:

"You should have returned them to me sooner, for I might have needed them."

She did open the jewel-box as her friend feared she would. If she should perceive the substitution, what would she think? What should she say? Would she take her for a robber?

Mrs. Loisel now knew the horrible life of necessity. She did her part, however, completely, heroically. It was necessary to pay this frightful debt. She would pay it. They sent away the maid; they changed her

9. **chaplet** [chap′ lit]: a string of jewels.
10. **louis** [lü′ ē]: a former French gold coin, worth 20 francs.

lodgings; they rented some rooms under a mansard[11] roof.

She learned the heavy cares of a household, the odious work of a kitchen. She washed the dishes, using her rosy nails upon the greasy pots and the bottoms of the stewpans. She washed the soiled linen, the chemises[12] and dishcloths, which she hung on the line to dry; she took down the refuse to the street each morning and brought up the water, stopping at each landing to breathe. And, clothed like a woman of the people, she went to the grocer's, the butcher's, and the fruiterer's, with her basket on her arm, shopping, haggling, defending to the last sou[13] her miserable money.

Every month it was necessary to renew some notes, thus obtaining time, and to pay others.

The husband worked evenings, putting the books of some merchants in order, and nights he often did copying at five sous a page.

And this life lasted for ten years.

At the end of ten years, they had restored all, all, with interest of the usurer, and accumulated interest besides.

Mrs. Loisel seemed old now. She had become a strong, hard woman, the crude woman of the poor household. Her hair badly dressed, her skirts awry, her hands red, she spoke in a loud tone, and washed the floors in large pails of water. But sometimes, when her husband was at the office, she would seat herself before the window and think of that evening party of former times, of that ball where she was so beautiful and so flattered.

How would it have been if she had not lost that necklace? Who knows? Who knows? How singular is life, and how full of changes! How small a thing will ruin or save one!

One Sunday, as she was taking a walk in the Champs-Elysèe[14] to rid herself of the cares of the week, she suddenly perceived a woman walking with a child. It was Mrs. Forestier, still young, still

---

a11. **mansard** [man′ särd]: a roof with two slopes on each side, named after the seventeenth-century French architect François Mansard.

12. **chemises** [shə mēz′ əz]: shirtlike undergarments for women and girls.

13. **sou** [sü]: a former French coin, worth 1/20 of a franc.

14. **Champs-Elysèe** [shäNs ā lē zē′]

In the Dining Room Berthe Morisot, 1886, oil on canvas, 24 1/8″ x 19 3/4″, National Gallery of Art, Washington, D. C. (Detail on page 99)

pretty, still attractive. Mrs. Loisel was affected. Should she speak to her? Yes, certainly. And now that she had paid, she would tell her all. Why not?

She approached her. "Good morning, Jeanne."

Her friend did not recognize her and was astonished to be so familiarly addressed by this common personage. She stammered:

"But, Madame—I do not know—You must be mistaken—"

"No, I am Matilda Loisel."

Her friend uttered a cry of astonishment: "Oh! my poor Matilda! How you have changed—"

"Yes, I have had some hard days

since I saw you; and some miserable ones—and all because of you—"

"Because of me? How is that?"

"You recall the diamond necklace that you loaned me to wear to the Commissioner's ball?"

"Yes, very well."

"Well, I lost it."

"How is that, since you returned it to me?"

"I returned another to you exactly like it. And it has taken us ten years to pay for it. You can understand that it was not easy for us who have nothing. But it is finished and I am decently content."

Madame Forestier stopped short. She said:

"You say that you bought a diamond necklace to replace mine?"

"Yes. You did not perceive it then? They were just alike."

And she smiled with a proud and simple joy. Madame Forestier was touched and took both her hands as she replied:

"Oh! my poor Matilda! Mine were false. They were not worth over five hundred francs!"

GUY DE MAUPASSANT

....

Guy de Maupassant (gē də mō pä säN´) (1850-1893) was born near Dieppe, in Normandy, France, and grew up in an unhappy home. His parents fought constantly and separated when he was twelve years old. The boy's interest in literature attracted the attention of a family friend, the author Gustave Flaubert, who advised the young writer all his life.

In 1870 the Franco-Prussian War began. By then de Maupassant was studying law in Paris, but rushed off to enlist. The devastating end of the war and the bitter civil war that followed had a strong influence on his writing. He took a tedious job he hated, but spent more and more time writing. Much of his work—the short stories for which he is famous—was published in magazines and newspapers of the time. Many of his stories, like "The Necklace," are famous for the twist in their endings.

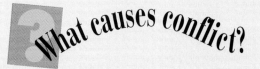

What causes conflict?

COMPARE Causes

Choose a literature selection from this unit. Then write a dialogue in which several characters from the selection debate the causes of the conflict. Have each individual state and defend a position on what has caused the conflict. Invite some classmates to perform your dialogue for your class.

LITERATURE STUDY

Plot

In stories, plays, and some poems, the **plot** is the actions and events of the story. Most plots have three main parts—*rising action*, *climax*, and *falling action*. The writer usually develops the conflict in the rising action.

For each story that you read in this unit, make a list of the plot events that reveal the conflict. List them in the order in which they happen. (*See "Plot" on page 119.*)

PLOT A LITERARY PLOT

The diagram on this page shows the rising action, climax, and falling action of "The Clearing." Select another story from this unit and diagram its plot. Mark the story's main events where they happen along the plot line.

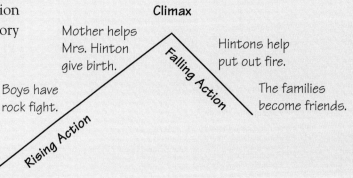

Climax

Mother helps Mrs. Hinton give birth.

Hintons help put out fire.

Boys have rock fight.

The families become friends.

Rising Action

Falling Action

What are the different kinds of conflict?

LITERATURE STUDY

Conflict

In literature, the struggle of the characters is called **conflict**. *External conflict* is caused by forces outside a character, such as another person, nature, or society. *Internal conflict* occurs when the character struggles with some inner feeling or quality, such as fear or aggression.

Conflict in a nonfiction account can also be internal or external. With a partner, select one of the nonfiction selections that you read in this unit and discuss whether the conflict it describes is internal, external, or a combination of both. (*See "Conflict" on page 118.*)

Investigate Idioms

With a small group, brainstorm expressions that describe conflict, such as *to hold a grudge* or *to be between a rock and a hard place*. Collect your expressions in a booklet for a classroom library resource. Then discuss which idioms could describe experiences in the literature selections that you read in this unit. For example, some readers might say that Scho in "A Game of Catch" has *a chip on his shoulder*.

Chart the Conflicts

In a small group, classify the conflict in each of the literature selections that you read in this unit by making a chart like this one. Then write a short explanation of why each selection belongs in its particular category.

Character against ...			
Character	**Society**	**Nature**	**Self**
"Get Up and Bar the Door"	"I Have a Dream"		

^Asking Big Questions About the Literature

How do individuals and groups resolve conflicts?

Find Out WHAT HAPPENED

Choose a conflict from one of the nonfiction selections that you've read. Then do some research to discover how people have continued trying to resolve this conflict. For example, have any parts of Martin Luther King, Jr.'s dream come true? If so, where? How fully? Keep track of your facts by making note cards like the one below. Then present your findings to the class as a special report.

Reference title: _____
Author's name: _____
Subject: Integration laws passed since 1963
Events: 1. _____
_____
2. _____
_____
3. _____
_____

LITERATURE STUDY

Conflict

In a work of literature, how a character resolves a **conflict** reveals the character's identity. Choose one of the stories you've read in this unit and write an essay about the main character's efforts to resolve the conflict. Explain the character's options for resolving the conflict, what the character decides to do, and what this choice reveals about him or her. (*See "Conflict" on page 118.*)

ROLE-PLAY Resolutions

With a group, think of a real-life conflict that resembles a conflict in a literature selection in this unit. For example, perhaps a new coach at your school has introduced changes, creating a conflict comparable to the one in "Umu Madu in the Good Old Days." Then role-play confrontations and resolutions between the two sides. Vote on which method best resolved the conflict.

What can people learn from conflict?

COMPARE & CONTRAST

Compare and contrast how two individuals your age have resolved a similar personal struggle. One should be a character from a literature selection in this unit. The other can be you or someone you know. Use a chart like the one below to help you write several paragraphs about the characters' similarities and differences.

LITERATURE STUDY

Plot

Choose one of the stories you've read in this unit. Now imagine the story if one of the events of the **plot** was changed. Rewrite the plot in outline form to show how this change would affect the story. *(See "Plot" on page 119.)*

Conflict	Character: Amanda	Me
Type	Internal (self against self)	Internal (self against self)
Subject	Wants to spend more time with mother.	Wants to spend more time with sister.
Causes	Mother is too busy.	Sister has boyfriend.
Resolution		

Hold A PANEL DISCUSSION

In a small group, let each member role-play a character from one of the literature selections in this unit. Each character should summarize his or her conflict. The class can then ask the characters questions about what they learned and what they might have done differently.

NOW Choose a Project!

Three projects that deal with conflict and resolution are described on the following pages. Choose the one that's right for you.

Writing Workshop

CONVINCE THEM WITH A LETTER

Wouldn't it be great to persuade two individuals or groups to resolve their conflict? This writing project will give you the chance to write a persuasive letter that will help others overcome their differences. The **purpose** of your persuasive letter will be to influence the opinions and actions of your **audience**, the people who are involved in this conflict. When you've sent your letter, you may find out how influential your words and ideas can really be.

Prewriting
THINK OF A CONFLICT

Read some letters to the editor in newspapers and magazines to give you ideas for local, national or international conflicts you'd like to write about. You'll soon get an idea of the kind of topics and issues that everyone is discussing.

When you have chosen a topic, ask yourself these questions.

- Is this a topic I have strong ideas about?
- Does this topic have more than one side?
- Can I find enough evidence to support my position?

Put yourself in your readers' place. Are your readers likely to agree or to disagree with your position? How well informed are they? Will you need to provide background information? What kind of evidence will convince them to agree with your position?

5207 Los Almos
SAN JOSE, NM 96341

January 20, 199—

Sarah Brown
Sun Times
1234 Main Street
Sunnyvale, NM 82970

Dear Ms. Brown,
    It bothers me that...

Anita Chavez
5207 Los Almos
San Jose, NM 96341

Sarah Brown Editor
Sun Times
1234 Main Street
Sunnyvale, NM 82970

Prewriting

DECIDE ON YOUR POSITION

Begin planning your persuasive letter by taking a stand. Write a clear thesis statement that states your main point and suggests a solution to the conflict.

In addition, summarize the main point of the opposing argument. Identifying the opposition's argument will show your readers that you've considered all sides of the issue.

The next step is to gather evidence that will support your position. Research to collect facts that will help make your argument convincing.

Finally map out your argument by making an informal outline. List the points you want to make, and be sure each one supports your thesis statement. Then list at least one piece of supporting evidence for each idea, like this:

Thesis statement: ————————————————

Point 1: ————————————————

Supporting evidence: ————————————————

Point 2: ————————————————

Supporting evidence: ————————————————

Point 3: ————————————————

Supporting evidence: ————————————————

Drafting
YOUR LETTER

Your outline will help you plan the basic structure of your argument. Be sure it includes the three essential parts—introduction, body, and conclusion.

- The introduction should explain the conflict, state your position, and suggest a resolution. Emily Johnson, a student writer, introduces her persuasive letter with a strong, clear thesis statement that states her position on gun control, "America needs stricter gun control laws . . ."

- The body should consist of one or more paragraphs that lead the reader logically through your main points. Be sure to support each point with evidence. For example, Emily presents statistics to show the low numbers of handgun murders in countries that have strict gun control laws. Her evidence adds support to her main point.

- Present the arguments of the opposition, to show that you have considered both sides of the issue. For example, Emily considers the argument that guns are necessary to defend the home. She then rejects this argument by presenting statistics showing that keeping a gun at home actually increases the possibility of murder.

- Write a conclusion that sums up your position and suggests a course of action. Emily, for example, ends her letter by calling for "stricter gun control laws, a waiting period for buying a gun, and more effective punishments for illegal gun suppliers."

Read Emily's argument on pages 110-111 for an example of a persuasive letter.

Revising
YOUR LETTER

Now test the persuasiveness of your letter on several class-mates. Their responses to questions such as these will help you polish your argument.

- Does the introduction present my position clearly?
- Is my argument clear and well supported?
- Which evidence is most convincing? Which is least convincing?
- Are there any opposing arguments I haven't mentioned?
- Did my argument persuade you?

Editing
YOUR LETTER

After you've revised your draft, work with a partner to edit your persuasive letter. Read one another's letters and check for errors in spelling, grammar, and punctuation. Mistakes could make your readers doubt the authority of your argument or the care of your research. Correct your errors and make a publishable copy of your letter.

Publishing
YOUR LETTER

Send your letter to those involved in the specific conflict, if possible, or send it to the editor of a local newspaper or magazine. You might read the letter at school, or else-where, as a speech—or even as part of a political campaign.

136 Old Mill Road
Framingham, MA 01701
March 3, 1994

Ms. Sarah Siddons
Editor
Daily Times
976 Main Street
Framingham, MA 01701

Dear Ms. Siddons:

America needs stricter gun control laws, such as a waiting period for buying guns to allow the police enough time to check the purchaser's criminal record. At the moment, Americans have easy access to these weapons. Many handgun owners, though, do not know how to use a gun properly. Nor do they know to keep guns away from children.

Opponents of gun control argue that "guns don't kill people—people kill people." This may be true, but a gun makes it much easier to kill someone. A gun may be a harmless object in itself, but when people use it to kill or hurt, shouldn't its use be controlled?

Opponents of gun control argue that guns are necessary to defend one's home against armed intruders. The truth is that having a gun in the house makes the possibility of killing someone who lives there three times greater. Gun supporters also argue that if the right to buy a gun is reduced or taken away, only criminals will have guns, purchased on the black market. Although some criminals do get guns on the black market, many don't need to when they can buy guns legally in a store. Making stricter regulations and punishments involving illegal selling of guns is a beginning to the solution of this many-sided problem.

Many people say that it is a question of freedom and argue that gun control is an attack on our constitutional rights. However, gun control is not the same as making all guns illegal and does not challenge our constitutional right to own a firearm. Gun control is not a violation of our rights—it is a moderation of them.

The statistics in favor of gun control are overwhelming. In males aged 17-24, handgun murder is the second most common cause of death. If guns were taken off the street, wouldn't it reduce the number of drive-by shootings? Controlling distribution of guns puts us one step closer to solving the problem of youth violence.

The following list reveals the number of handgun murders in countries with strict gun control laws compared to the handgun murder rate in the United States during 1990: Australia—10 deaths; Sweden—18; Great Britain—22; Canada—68; Japan—87; Switzerland—91; The UNITED STATES—10,567. These numbers are evidence of our country's problem.

How can we ignore the obvious? The arguments against guns far outweigh the arguments in favor of them. We need stricter gun control laws, a waiting period for buying a gun, and more effective punishments for illegal gun suppliers. When the number of guns on the street is reduced, maybe we can feel safer in our cities, our towns, and our homes.

Sincerely,

Emily Johnson

Emily Johnson

Cooperative Learning

A TV GUIDE FOR PARENTS

Situation comedies on TV are mostly about the assorted struggles people experience in daily life. Viewers can observe the characters dealing with ordinary problems week after week and surviving with spirit and humor.

All "sitcoms" aren't instructive in positive ways, though. Some show characters coasting in and out of conflict through negative behavior such as deception. These programs may not offer good role models for younger children. That's where you can help. You and your small group will develop a TV guide for parents of elementary students who want to supervise their kids' TV watching.

The
RATING PROCESS

Use a weekly TV guide to make a list of prime-time situation comedies in your area. Each person in your group should then choose two or three shows to watch and evaluate. To be fair in making your evaluations, track each show over several weeks with the help of the evaluation sheet on the facing page.

good

TV Viewing
for
Elementary School
Kids

T V Show_____	Dates_____
Plot	• Summarize the plot of a typical episode. • What types of conflict does the show usually depict? Who or what causes them? • What sort of thing tends to happen in the last scene?
Characters	• Are the characters types, or are they like real people? • What strategies do the characters use to solve their problems? • Do the characters learn from their conflicts, or do they make similar choices and mistakes each week?
Theme	• What do the writers of this program seem to believe about people? What lessons or values does their show express?
Conclusions	• What did you like and dislike about the program? • Does this show provide positive or negative role models?
Recommendation	• Do you recommend this program for young children?

The PUBLICATION

Now assign the roles of Secretary, Copy Writer, Designers, Editor, and Proofreader to the members of your group. The Secretary will collect everyone's evaluation sheets and order them according to the times on the TV schedule. The Copy Writer will write an introduction that explains the purpose and standards of the guide. Then the Editor will check for errors in usage, punctuation, and spelling. Next the Secretary can type or neatly rewrite the pages. While Designers create a cover, the Proofreader can check the pages for errors.

The PRESENTATION

With your teacher's help, arrange a time to present your TV guide to an elementary school principal or teacher for distribution to parents. Make as many copies of the guide as you need, and staple or put them in folders. Then get ready to be thanked for all your guidance and hard work!

Helping Your Community

Since people are individuals with different experiences, values, and beliefs, we can't reasonably hope to eliminate all conflict from the planet. But you and a small group can make a difference on a smaller scale. By teaching conflict management skills in a specially developed manual, you can help others—such as two groups of people in your town—develop the skills they need for settling disagreements peacefully.

Designing
PART ONE

For this first section of your conflict resolution manual, brainstorm with your group all the general behavior strategies that help people solve disputes. Consider your own experiences as well as those of characters in the literature selections for this unit. Think of strategies people need in all kinds of conflict situations, from a playground scuffle to a parent-teenager argument over a curfew. Keep in mind that readers will need many strategies in order to resolve different kinds of conflict and that the resolution of a single conflict often requires several strategies. List your strategies under big headings such as *Speaking*, *Listening*, and *Negotiating*.

"Couldn't we try mediation?"

Next, work with your group to write explanations and examples to go with each strategy on your lists. For instance, to help people avoid blaming each other, you might explain that wording statements about wants and needs with "I…" rather than "You…" can prevent the other party from feeling blamed or accused. Keep your explanations and examples brief, clear, and as useful in real life as possible.

Designing PART TWO

In the second part of your conflict resolution manual, focus on a specific community issue that your group can help resolve. For example, merchants and chalk artists in your town may be at odds over who can decorate the sidewalk, or a neighborhood may say it needs a park that the city says it can't afford. As you write this section, be sure not to take sides on the issue. Fairly summarize both sides, and suggest possible compromises. Where it might help, refer your readers to conflict resolution methods in Part One, suggesting how certain methods can be used in this case.

Publishing YOUR MANUAL

Whether you produce your manual by handwriting or by typing doesn't really matter, but a neat, error-free guide does. Once you've polished and proofread, supply copies to the local groups you targeted in Part Two. You could also offer your work to the school, the town council, or any other group needing conflict mediation.

Putting It All Together

What Have You Learned About the Theme?

Now that you've read *Out of Tune*, completed the activities, and created a project, think about what you've learned. Review all the writing you've done for this unit. Then—to see whether your ideas about conflict resolution have changed—write an essay comparing and contrasting how you resolved a conflict in the past with how you'd resolve it today.

PAST AND PRESENT

Prewriting   Think of a conflict you once needed to resolve, such as a disagreement with someone you cared about or a hard decision. It doesn't matter whether the result was positive or negative, as long as you remember the details. Then think about how you would resolve the same problem today. If necessary, make a Venn diagram to sort out the similarities and differences.

Drafting   Begin by summarizing the conflict. Don't try to narrate the entire thing; just explain the issue, the cause of the conflict, the methods you used to resolve it, and the outcome. In a second paragraph, explain how you'd deal with the same situation now. Then write a concluding paragraph about why you think your past and present methods for resolving the conflict are different. Did you learn anything new about conflict resolution from a particular literature selection or an activity in this unit? If your methods haven't changed, explain what literature or projects in this unit reinforced your ideas about how to resolve conflict.

Now go back and write a topic sentence and an introduction to your essay.

Revising, Proofreading, and Publishing   As you revise your essay, be sure that it supports the major point expressed in your topic sentence. Your summary of the original conflict, your explanation of how you'd resolve it today, and the conclusion you draw should support and clarify this main idea. Once you've proofread for errors in grammar, usage, punctuation, and spelling, give copies of your essay to the members of a group that you worked with in this unit.

Evaluating Your Work

Think Back About the Big Questions

With a partner, discuss the Big Questions on pages 10-11. Do you have trouble answering any of these questions now? Write some sentences about how your answers to the Big Questions have changed as a result of your work in this unit.

Think Back About Your Work

Now evaluate your work, including your reading, your writing, your activities, and your projects. On another page, answer the following questions. Add your name. Then give your evaluation to your teacher.

- How have your ideas about conflict resolution changed? What literature selections or activities in this unit contributed to the change? If your ideas stayed the same, what parts of the unit reinforced them?

- Which literature selections would you recommend to your friends? Explain.

- What were your favorite activities? Why?

- What part of your project did you enjoy most?

- What kind of activity or project would you have liked to see in the unit? Explain.

- In one sentence, sum up the importance of conflict resolution.

- How do you rate your work in this unit? (Be honest and fair to yourself.) Use the following scale. Then explain why you chose that number.

  1=Outstanding   3=Fair

  2=Good   4=Not as good as it could have been

CONFLICT

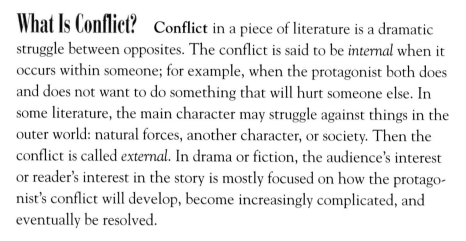

What Is Conflict?

Conflict in a piece of literature is a dramatic struggle between opposites. The conflict is said to be *internal* when it occurs within someone; for example, when the protagonist both does and does not want to do something that will hurt someone else. In some literature, the main character may struggle against things in the outer world: natural forces, another character, or society. Then the conflict is called *external*. In drama or fiction, the audience's interest or reader's interest in the story is mostly focused on how the protagonist's conflict will develop, become increasingly complicated, and eventually be resolved.

Requesting and Offering Advice   Imagine that you are someone facing some kind of conflict. This conflict could be internal or external. Then write a letter to the advice column of a newspaper, explaining the conflict. Address the letter to yourself. Then switch roles and imagine you are the advice columnist. Write a response to your first letter, suggesting ways of resolving the conflict.

Role-Playing a Solution   With a partner, select two characters from a short story selection in this unit whose conflict you found especially interesting. Then imagine a different kind of conflict that these two characters might experience. Discuss how the characters might resolve this conflict. It might help your discussion if you remember how these characters dealt with their conflict in the story. Was it easy or difficult for them to resolve their problem? Role-play their interaction for your class, beginning with their conflict and ending with the conflict's resolution.

What Is Plot?

Plot in literature is the order of events in a work of narrative fiction, poetry, or drama. Usually the plot develops in three main stages. The first stage is called the *rising action,* in which the main character's circumstances are introduced and become increasingly complicated. The second stage is called the *climax,* when the character's conflict or predicament becomes most intense or changes drastically. The last stage is called the *falling action,* which resolves the complicated situation. In some cases, the plot concludes with a *reversal* of the protagonist's circumstances, based on some startling discovery.

Writing a Poem   Create a *diamante,* a seven-line poem with a certain number of words in each line (1-2-3-4-3-2-1) that contains a shift in meaning in the middle. Plan your poem so that its first three lines suggest an intensifying feeling of conflict, the fourth line sugggests a climax or change in that intensity, and the last three lines express a feeling that the conflict is resolved. Show your poem to a friend.

> Arguing
> Night wind:
> Wailing, wakening, flailing,
> Flashing light! Then thunder,
> Dark rain, swift
> Drifting cloud,
> Sleep.
> —H.B.

Writing an Essay   Using an outline to help you organize your ideas, write an essay comparing and contrasting the causes, complications, and resolution of a conflict you've had with those of a conflict in a literature selection in this unit. Draw some conclusions about the differences and similarities you've identified.

GLOSSARY OF LITERARY TERMS

alliteration Repetition of the first sound—usually a consonant sound—in several words of a sentence or a line of poetry.

allusion An author's indirect reference to someone or something that is presumed to be familiar to the reader.

anecdote A short narrative about an interesting or a humorous event, usually in the life of a person.

antagonist The person or force opposing the protagonist, or main character in a literary work. [See also *protagonist*.]

autobiography A person's written account of his or her own life.

B

ballad A poem, often a song, that tells a story in simple verse.

biography An account of a person's life, written by another person.

blank verse Unrhymed poetry.

C

character A person or an animal that participates in the action of a work of literature. A *dynamic character* is one whose thoughts, feelings, and actions are changeable and lifelike; a *static character* always remains the same. [See also *protagonist, antagonist.*]

characterization The creation of characters through the characters' use of language and through descriptions of their appearance, thoughts, emotions, and actions. [See also *character.*]

chronology An arrangement of events in the order in which they happen.

cliché An overused expression that is trite rather than meaningful.

climax The highest point of tension in the plot of a work of literature. [See also *plot*.]

comedy An amusing play that has a happy ending.

conclusion The final part or ending of a piece of literature.

concrete poem A poem arranged on the page so that its punctuation, letters, and lines make the shape of the subject of the poem.

conflict A problem that confronts the characters in a piece of literature. The conflict may be *internal* (a character's struggle within himself or herself) or *external* (a character's struggle against nature, another person, or society). [See also *plot*.]

context The general sense of words that helps readers to understand the meaning of unfamiliar words and phrases in a piece of writing.

D

description An author's use of words to give the reader or listener a mental picture, an impression, or an understanding of a person, place, thing, event, or idea.

dialect A form of speech spoken by people in a particular group or geographical region that differs in vocabulary, grammar, and pronunciation from the standard language.

dialogue The spoken words and conversation of characters in a work of literature.

drama A play that is performed before an audience according to stage directions and using dialogue. Classical drama has two genres: *tragedy* and *comedy*. Modern drama includes *melodrama, satire, theater of the absurd,* and *pantomime*. [See also *comedy, play,* and *tragedy*.]

dramatic poetry A play written in the form of poetry.

E

epic A long narrative poem—written in a formal style and meant to be read aloud—that relates the adventures and experiences of one or more great heroes or heroines.

essay   Personal nonfiction writing about a particular subject that is important to the writer.

excerpt   A passage from a larger work that has been taken out of its context to be used for a special purpose.

exposition   Writing that explains, analyzes, or defines.

extended metaphor   An elaborately drawn out metaphor. [See also *metaphor*.]

F

fable   A short, simple story whose purpose is to teach a lesson, usually with animal characters who talk and act like people.

fantasy   Imaginative fiction about unrealistic characters, places, and events.

fiction   Literature, including the short story and the novel, that tells about imaginary people and events.

figurative language Language used to express ideas through figures of speech: descriptions that aren't meant to be taken literally. Types of figurative language include *simile, metaphor, extended metaphor, hyperbole,* and *personification*.

figure of speech   A type of figurative language, not meant to be taken literally, that expresses something in such a way that it brings the thing to life in the reader's or listener's imagination. [See also *figurative language*.]

flashback   A break in a story's action that relates a past happening in order to give the reader background information about a present action in the story.

folktale   A story that has been passed along from storyteller to storyteller for generations. Kinds of folktales include *tall tales, fairy tales, fables, legends,* and *myths.*

foreshadowing   The use of clues to create suspense by giving the reader or audience hints of events to come.

free verse   Poetry that has no formal rhyme scheme or metrical pattern.

G

genre   A major category of art. The three major literary genres are poetry, prose, and drama.

H

haiku   A three-line Japanese verse form. In most haiku, the first and third lines have five syllables, while the second line has seven. The

traditional haiku describes a complicated feeling or thought in simple language through a single image.

hero/heroine   The main character in a work of literature. In heroic literature, the hero or heroine is a particularly brave, noble, or clever person whose achievements are unusual and important. [See also *character.*]

heroic age   The historical period in western civilization—from about 800 B.C. through A.D. 200—during which most works of heroic literature, such as myths and epics, were created in ancient Greece and Rome.

hubris   Arrogance or excessive pride leading to mistakes; the character flaw in a hero of classical tragedy.

hyperbole   An obvious exaggeration used for emphasis. [See also *figurative language*.]

I

idiom   An expression whose meaning cannot be understood from the ordinary meaning of the words. For example, *It's raining cats and dogs.*

imagery   The words and phrases in writing that appeal to the senses of sight, hearing, taste, touch, and smell.

irony   An effect created by a sharp contrast between what is expected and what is real. An *ironic twist* in a plot is an event that is the complete opposite of what the characters have been hoping or expecting will happen. An *ironic statement* declares the opposite of the speaker's literal meaning.

J

jargon   Words and phrases used by a group of people who share the same profession or special interests in order to refer to technical things or processes with which they are familiar. In general, jargon is any terminology that sounds unclear, overused, or pretentious.

L

legend   A famous folktale about heroic actions, passed along by word of mouth from generation to generation. The legend may have begun as a factual account of real people and events but has become mostly or completely fictitious.

limerick   A form of light verse, or humorous poetry, written in one five-line stanza with a regular scheme of rhyme and meter.

literature   The branch of art that is expressed in written language and includes all written genres.

lyric poem   A short poem that expresses personal feelings and thoughts in a musical way. Originally, lyrics were the words of songs that were sung to music played on the lyre, a stringed instrument invented by the ancient Greeks.

M

metamorphosis   The transformation of one thing, or being, into another completely different thing or being, such as a caterpillar's change into a butterfly.

metaphor   Figurative language in which one thing is said to be another thing. [See also *figurative language*.]

meter   The pattern of rhythm in lines of poetry. The most common meter, in poetry written in English, is iambic pentameter, that is, a verse having five metrical feet, each foot of verse having two syllables, an unaccented one followed by an accented one.

mood   The feeling or atmosphere that a reader senses while reading or listening to a work of literature.

motivation   A character's reasons for doing, thinking, feeling, or saying something. Sometimes an author will make a character's motivation obvious from the beginning. In realistic fiction and drama, however, a character's motivation may be so complicated that the reader discovers it gradually, by studying the character's thoughts, feelings, and behavior.

myth   A story, passed along by word of mouth for generations, about the actions of gods and goddesses or superhuman heroes and heroines. Most myths were first told to explain the origins of natural things or to justify the social rules and customs of a particular society.

N

narration   The process of telling a story. For both fiction and nonfiction, there are two main kinds of narration, based on whether the story is told from a first-person or third-person point of view. [See also *point of view*.]

narrative poem   A poem that tells a story containing the basic literary ingredients of fiction: character, setting, and plot.

narrator   The person, or voice, that tells a story. [See also *point of view, voice*.]

nonfiction   Prose that is factually true and is about real people, events, and places.

nonstandard English
Versions of English, such as slang and dialects, that use pronunciation, vocabulary, idiomatic expressions, grammar, and punctuation that differ from the accepted "correct" constructions of English.

novel   A long work of narrative prose fiction. A novel contains narration, a setting or settings, characters, dialogue, and a more complicated plot than a short story.

O

onomatopoeia   The technique of using words that imitate the sounds they describe, such as *hiss*, *buzz*, and *splash*.

oral tradition   Stories, poems, and songs that have been kept alive by being told, recited, and sung by people over many generations. Since the works were not originally written, they often have many different versions.

P

parable   A brief story—similar to a fable, but about people—that describes an ordinary situation and concludes with a short moral or lesson to be learned.

personification   Figurative language in which an animal, an object, or an idea is given human characteristics. [See also *figurative language*.]

persuasion   A type of speech or writing whose purpose is to convince people that something is true or important.

play   A work of dramatic literature written for performance by actors before an audience. In classical or traditional drama, a play is divided into five acts, each containing a number of scenes. Each act represents a distinct phase in the development of the plot. Modern plays often have only one act and one scene.

playwright   The author of a play.

plot   The sequence of actions and events in fiction or drama. A traditional plot has at least three parts: the *rising action*, leading up to a turning point that affects the main character; the *climax*, the turning point or moment of greatest intensity or interest; and the *falling action*, leading away from the conflict, or resolving it.

poetry   Language selected and arranged in order to say something in a compressed or nonliteral way. Modern poetry may or may not use many of the traditional poetic techniques that include *meter*, *rhyme*, *alliteration*, *figurative language*, *symbolism*, and *specific verse forms*.

point of view   The perspective from which a writer tells a story. *First-person* narrators tell the story from their own point of view, using pronouns such as *I* or *me*. *Third-person* narrators, using pronouns such as *he*, *she*, or *them*, may be *omniscient* (knowing everything about all characters), or *limited* (taking the point of view of one character). [See also *narration*.]

propaganda   Information or ideas that may or may not be true, but are spread as though they are true, in order to persuade people to do or believe something.

prose   The ordinary form of written and spoken language used to create fiction, nonfiction, and most drama.

protagonist   The main character of a literary work. [See also *character* and *characterization*.]

R

refrain   A line or group of lines that is repeated, usually at the end of each verse, in a poem or a song.

repetition   The use of the same formal element more than once in a literary work, for emphasis or in order to achieve another desired effect.

resolution   The falling action in fiction or drama,

including all of the developments that follow the climax and show that the story's conflict is over. [See also *plot*.]

rhyme scheme   A repeated pattern of similar sounds, usually found at the ends of lines of poetry or poetic drama.

rhythm   In poetry, the measured recurrence of accented and unaccented syllables in a particular pattern. [See also *meter*.]

S

scene   The time, place, and circumstances of a play or a story. In a play, a scene is a section of an act. [See also *play*.]

science fiction   Fantasy literature set in an imaginary future, with details and situations that are designed to seem scientifically possible.

setting   The time and place of a work of literature.

short story   Narrative prose fiction that is shorter and has a less complicated plot than a novel. A short story contains narration, at least one setting, at least one character, and usually some dialogue.

simile   Figurative language that compares two unlike things, introduced by the words "like" or "as." [See also *figurative language*.]

soliloquy   In a play, a short speech spoken by a single character when he or she is alone on the stage. A soliloquy usually expresses the character's innermost thoughts and feelings, when he or she thinks no other characters can hear.

sonnet   A poem written in one stanza, using fourteen lines of iambic pentameter. [See also *meter*.]

speaker   In poetry, the individual whose voice seems to be speaking the lines. [See also *narration, voice*.]

stage directions   The directions, written by the playwright, to tell the director, actors, and theater technicians how a play should be dramatized. Stage directions may specify such things as how the setting should appear in each scene, how the actors should deliver their lines, when the stage curtain should rise and fall, how stage lights should be used, where on the stage the actors should be during the action, and when sound effects should be used.

stanza   A group of lines in poetry set apart by blank lines before and after the group; a poetic verse.

style   The distinctive way in which an author composes a work of literature in written or spoken language.

suspense   An effect created by authors of various types of fiction and drama, especially adventure and mystery, to heighten interest in the story.

symbol   An image, person, place, or thing that is used to express the idea of something else.

T

tall tale   A kind of folk tale, or legend, that exaggerates the characteristics of its hero or heroine.

theme   The main idea or underlying subject of a work of literature.

tone   The attitude that a work of literature expresses to the reader through its style.

tragedy   In classical drama, a tragedy depicts a noble hero or heroine who makes a mistake of judgment that has disastrous consequences.

V

verse   A stanza in a poem. Also, a synonym for poetry as a genre. [See also *stanza*.]

voice   The narrator or the person who relates the action of a piece of literature. [See also *speaker*.]

ACKNOWLEDGMENTS

Grateful acknowledgment is made for permission to reprint the following copyrighted material.

"Amanda and the Wounded Birds" by Colby Rodowsky, copyright © 1987 by Colby Rodowsky, from *Visions* by Donald R. Gallo, Editor. Used by permission of Dell Books, a division of Bantam Doubleday Dell Publishing Group, Inc.

"Danielle O'Mara" from *Class Dismissed II* by Mel Glenn. Text copyright © 1986 by Mel Glenn. Reprinted by permission of Clarion Books/Houghton Mifflin Co. All rights reserved.

"A Game of Catch" by Richard Wilbur is reprinted by permission from *Stories From The New Yorker 1950-1960,* copyright © 1960 by the *New Yorker Magazine, Inc.* Published by Simon and Schuster.

"Umu Madu in the Good Old Days" from *How Tables Came to Umu Madu* by T. Obinkaram Echewa. Reprinted by permission of the author.

"The Clearing" by Jesse Stuart. "The Clearing" by Jesse Stuart appeared originally in Ladies' Home Journal. Copyright 1954 by Jesse Stuart. Copyright © renewed 1982 Jesse Stuart Foundation. Reprinted by permission of the Jesse Stuart Foundation, P.O. Box 391, Ashland KY 41114.

"The Long Way Around" by Jean McCord from *Deep Where the Octopi Lie,* copyright ©1968 by Jean McCord. Reprinted by permission of the author.

"I Have a Dream" by Martin Luther King, Jr., is reprinted by arrangement with The Heirs to the Estate of Martin Luther King, Jr., c/o Joan Daves Agency as agent for the proprietor. Copyright © 1963 by Martin Luther King, Jr., copyright renewed 1991 by Coretta Scott King.

"Shells" by Cynthia Rylant. Reprinted with the permission of Bradbury Press, an Affiliate of Macmillan, Inc. from *Every Living Thing* by Cynthia Rylant. Copyright ©1985 by Cynthia Rylant.

"The Silent Lobby" by Mildred Pitts Walter. Copyright © 1990 by Mildred Pitts Walter. Reprinted by permission of the author.

"The Fuller Brush Man" by Gloria D. Miklowitz, copyright © 1987 by Gloria D. Miklowitz, from *Visions* by Donald R. Gallo, Editor. Used by permission of Dell Books, a division of Bantam Doubleday Dell Publishing Group, Inc.

"Brown vs. Board of Education" by Walter Dean Myers from *Now Is Your Time! : The African-American Struggle for Freedom,* copyright © 1991 by Walter Dean Myers. Reprinted by permission of HarperCollins Publishers.

PHOTOGRAPHY

4 *l* John Owens/©D.C. Heath; *r* Sandy Roessler/The Stock Market; **5** Lois Schlowsky Computer Imagery. Photo of Martin Luther King, Jr., by Bob`Adelman/Magnum Photos, Inc.; **6** Richard Haynes/©D.C. Heath; **8** *t* Robert Brenner/PhotoEdit; *b* Pamela Schuyler/Stock Boston; **9** *t* John Eastcott/Stock Boston; *b* Alan Oddie/PhotoEdit; **10** *t* Sarah Putnam/©D.C. Heath; *b* Julie Bidwell/©D.C. Heath; **11** *t* Skjold/The Image Works; *c* Jim Whitmer/Stock Boston; *b* Tony Freeman/PhotoEdit; **12-13** Rare Books Division, Library of Congress; **17** ©Photo R.M.N. ©SPADEM Paris/Artists Rights Society, New York, 1994; **21** Photo by Sally Foster. Courtesy of Farrar, Straus and Giroux, Inc.; **22** Harriet Gans/The Image Works; **23** Courtesy of Clarion Books; **24-27** Lois Schlowsky Computer Imagery. Photos of tree and baseball player by Gayna Hoffman; **29** Photo by Constance Stuart Larrabee. Courtesy of Harcourt Brace and Company; **30-37** *border* From the Girard Foundation Collection in the Museum of International Folk Art, a unit of the Museum of New Mexico. Photo by Michel Montaux; **31** Sally Mayman/Tony Stone Images; **34-35** Bruno Barbey/Magnum Photos; **38-39, 40-41** *detail*, **43** *detail* United Missouri Bank, Kansas City. ©Thomas Hart Benton/VAGA, NY, 1995. Photo by Robert Newcombe; **45** The Jesse Stuart Foundation; **46-52** Ralph Mercer Photography/©D.C. Heath; **56-57** Lois Schlowsky Computer Imagery. Photo of children by David Young-Wolff/PhotoEdit. Photo of Martin Luther King, Jr., by Bob Adelman/Magnum Photos, Inc.; **61** Howard Frank/Personality Photos; **62** José Luis Grande/Photo Researchers; **65, 66-67** *t* Tom McHugh/Allstock; **67** *b* Courtesy of Macmillan Children's Book Group; **68** The Bettmann Archive; **70-71** *background* The Bettman Archive; **74-75** UPI/Bettmann; **75** *b* Courtesy of Macmillan Children's Book Group; **76-81** R.P. Kingston/Stock Boston; **81** *inset* Sandy Weiner. Courtesy of Bantam Doubleday Dell; **82, 85** Collection of Michael D. Davis; **86** UPI/Bettmann; **88** Collection of the Supreme Court of the United States; **89** Courtesy of HarperCollins Publishers; **90-91** ©Terje Rakke/The Image Bank; **92, 96** *detail* The Metropolitan Museum of Art. Gift of Katrin S. Vietor, in loving memory of Ernest G. Vietor, 1960. (60.174); **99** *detail,* **100** Chester Dale Collection. ©1993 National Gallery of Art, Washington; **103** Nancy Sheehan/©DC Heath; **106** *t* Elizabeth Hamlin/Stock Boston; *b* Ken O'Donoghue/©D.C. Heath; **108** Peanuts cartoon reprinted by permission of UFS, Inc.; **112** Jean-Claude Lejeune/Stock Boston; **114** *t* © J. Sulley/The Image Works; *b* ©1993 Peter Steiner and the Cartoon Bank, Inc.

Back cover *t* Sarah Putnam/©D.C. Heath; *c* John Owens/©D.C. Heath; *b* Julie Bidwell/©D.C. Heath.

Full Pronunciation Key for Footnoted Words

(Each pronunciation and definition is adapted from *Scott, Foresman Advanced Dictionary* by E.L. Thorndike and Clarence L. Barnhart.)

The pronunciation of each footnoted word is shown just after the word, in this way: **abbreviate** [ə brē′ vē āt]. The letters and signs used are pronounced as in the words below. The mark ′ is placed after a syllable with primary or heavy accent, as in the example above. The mark ′ after a syllable shows a secondary or lighter accent, as in **abbreviation** [ə brē′ vē ā′ shən].

Some words, taken from foreign languages, are spoken with sounds that do not otherwise occur in English. Symbols for these sounds are given in the key as "foreign sounds."

a	hat, cap	j	jam, enjoy	u	cup, butter	**foreign sounds**
ā	age, face	k	kind, seek	u̇	full, put	
ä	father, far	l	land, coal	ü	rule, move	Y as in French *du*.

a hat, cap
ā age, face
ä father, far

b bad, rob
ch child, much
d did, red

e let, best
ē equal, be
ėr term, learn

f fat, if
g go, bag
h he, how

i it, pin
ī ice, five

j jam, enjoy
k kind, seek
l land, coal
m me, am
n no, in
ng long, bring

o hot, rock
ō open, go
ô order, all
oi oil, voice
ou house, out

p paper, cup
r run, try
s say, yes
sh she, rush
t tell, it
th thin, both
ŦH then, smooth

u cup, butter
u̇ full, put
ü rule, move
v very, save
w will, woman
y young, yet
z zero, breeze
zh measure, seizure

ə represents:
   a in about
   e in taken
   i in pencil
   o in lemon
   u in circus

foreign sounds

Y as in French *du*. Pronounce (ē) with the lips rounded as for (ü).

à as in French *ami*. Pronounce (ä) with the lips spread and held tense.

œ as in French *peu*. Pronounce (ā) with the lips rounded as for (ō).

N as in French *bon*. The N is not pronounced, but shows that the vowel before it is nasal.

H as in German *ach*. Pronounce (k) without closing the breath passage.